THOSE GALLANT MEN

THOSE GALLANT MEN

On Trial in Vietnam

John Stevens Berry

★
PRESIDIO

Copyright © 1984 by Presidio Press
Published by Presidio Press, 31 Pamaron Way, Novato, CA 94947

Library of Congress Cataloging in Publication Data

Berry, John Stevens, 1938–
    Those gallant men.

    1. Trials (Military offenses)—United States.
    2. Courts-martial and courts of inquiry—United States.
    3. Berry, John Stevens, 1938–   .   4. Vietnamese
    Conflict, 1961–1975—Personal narratives, American.
    I. Title
    KF7641.B47   1984   343.73'0143   83-24736
    ISBN 0-89141-186-0   347.303143

"A Dream Vision," from *Collected Poems* by Yvor Winters
(Swallow Press, 1960), reprinted with the permission of
Ohio University Press, Athens.

Lines from "Like Decorations in a Nigger Cemetary"
by Wallace Stevens, reprinted from *Collected Poems*
with permission of Alfred A. Knopf, Inc.

Lines from "Gerontion" by T. S. Eliot, reprinted from
Collected Poems with permission of Harcourt Brace Jovanovitch.

Lines from "Round" by Weldon Kees, reprinted from
The Collected Poems of Weldon Kees by permission of University of
Nebraska Press, copyright © 1975 by the University of Nebraska Press.

Photo credits: Frontispiece photos with permission of
World Wide Photos

DEDICATION

*This book was written for Margaret and for our children:
Laura, John, Christopher, and Rory.*

*It is dedicated to the memory of my parents: Glenn Welty Berry
(1898–1966 and Susan Blanche Stevens Berry (1904–1974)
who lived in Onawa, Iowa.*

*And to those lawyers from my family and my wife's family
who have practiced law in Iowa and Nebraska:*

Frank A. Berry (1860–1912)   *Wade Stevens (1896–1983)*
John A. Berry (1862–1954)   *Ray N. Berry (1902–1968)*
John Stevens (1871–1958)   *Kenneth L. Noha (1948–1973)*
Fred S. Berry (1879–1948)   *Thomas A. Berry (1941–)*

IN MEMORIAM

SP/5 John W. Stevens (1945–1968)
Lt. Col. Robert W. Jones (1932–1980)
Walter N. Andersen (1915(1979)

. . . I was wounded in the house of my friends.

—*Zech. 13:6*

Contents

Foreword

This book is "must" reading for anyone interested in the administration of justice in the military. I also recommend it to anyone interested in justice in general.

Only someone who has participated in a military court-martial knows how hard it is to achieve a favorable result for the accused. Steve Berry shows the reader how, through efforts of lawyers like him, the military judicial system effectively protects the rights of accused persons.

Vietnam meant many things to many people. To Steve Berry, however, it was just another forum where he could ply his trade. The courtrooms were sometimes tents, or shacks, or bunkers, however, and he and his fellow military lawyers came to court carrying side arms along with their briefcases. While the stage and the props were different, the end result was Justice.

Mr. Berry is a Fellow of the American Board of Criminal Lawyers, a national honorary organization open by invitation to outstanding criminal trial lawyers. We are proud that he could take the time from his practice to write this book.

J. William Gallup
President, American Board of Criminal Lawyers

Introduction

I had heard of Captain Berry before I met him. It was, I had heard, as if the Welsh poet Dylan Thomas had slipped into a set of jungle fatigues and had set out to work his magic on behalf of all the accused in Vietnam.

And I had heard other things about him. I had heard that he had (like myself) voluntarily come to Vietnam; I had heard that he had previously filled his military obligation as an infantry officer, that he had spent a few very successful years as a civilian trial lawyer, and that he had felt a special calling to come to Vietnam to represent the GIs in trouble.

My duties were not primarily those of a defense counsel, and my office was at Long Binh. Steve Berry was a defense counsel who traveled to any place in Vietnam where he could find a case to try. It is possible that we would never have met but for the Green Beret case. It has always been my opinion that the fact the charges were ever filed against Col. Robert Rheault and his fellow Green Beret officers was a tragedy for the United States Army, as well as for my client, Bob Rheault. But out of this tragedy came an opportunity I had to work with Steve Berry, and Bill Hart—as well as Henry Rothblatt, Edward Bennett Williams, and other renowned criminal lawyers.

In Berry's book he does tell about the Green Beret case, but he tells much more than that. He gives a bird's-eye view of the criminal justice system as it actually functioned in Vietnam. He writes with wisdom and compassion, and everywhere in this book I find evidence of that fierce intellect that made him a feared cross-examiner and gave him a theater-wide reputation as defense counsel.

The experience of knowing Steve Berry in Vietnam was rich and rewarding in every sense of those words—he was at once a poet and a gladiator, an idealist, and a hard-nosed country lawyer. He was known for being absolutely fearless, in the court-room as well as outside of it. His book reflects the depth and breadth of the Captain Berry I knew. Every page is filled with the compassion and generosity that marked him as a man and a lawyer—and now as an author.

The Honorable Martin J. Linsky
Federal Administrative Law Judge

Acknowledgments

This book was written in the midst of a very busy law practice. It could not have been written without the friendship, loyalty, and support of my law firm. Many thanks to the attorneys and staff of BERRY ANDERSON CREAGER & WITTSTRUCK of Lincoln, Nebraska.

When I first began to write the book, it became apparent that I would need access to much information that was classified secret, or higher. It took me several years to get all the information needed, and I was assisted in no small way by the good offices of Sen. Edward Zorinsky and his staff, who went out of their way to help me get materials. Similarly, I received cooperation from the Office of the Judge Advocate General. Those offices provided me with literally thousands of pages of documents (including the letters various citizens wrote to the president and other officials regarding the Green Beret case), and I am grateful for their efforts. I have had serious disagreements with some of the highest-ranking members of the Judge Advocate General's Corps, but I remain firm in my conviction that the corps is the world's largest and best law firm—I am proud to have been a member of that organization.

There were a number of people who would have preferred that I not write this book at all. Among them were Col. Bob Rheault (U.S.A. Ret.), Col. Leland Brumley who is still on active duty, and former Maj. Budge Williams. When all of them were convinced that I would go ahead with the book irrespective of their wishes that I "scrub" it, each of them worked hard to provide me with accurate information. I have tapes, letters, and taped telephone conversations in which they graciously participated. They went out of their ways to help me write a book they would have preferred not to have been written. Another retired officer, Col. Bill Simpson, assisted me with background information. (Any reader who would like a deeper and clearer understanding of the function and mission of the Special Forces should read Bill's book, *Inside the Green Berets: The First Thirty Years*, which was based in part on the manuscript of a book Bob Rheault had written and then abandoned.) Marty Linsky and Bill Hart donated valuable time in reading and commenting on my manuscript, and Nan Rheault not only provided important information but also loaned me her scrapbook filled with the coverage the international press had given to the Green Beret case.

I had set out to write a book about all the cases I had tried while I was in Vietnam. I could not remember the names of many of those cases, but as to the ones I could remember, I sent away to the Department of the Army for records of trial. In all but the Green Beret case, the army was able to comply whenever I could adequately identify the name of my client. There were, of course, many clients whose names I simply could not remember. My initial efforts at putting together a book produced a manuscript several hundred thousand words long. My good friend, Prof. Mary Daehler Smith of Nebraska Wesleyan University, helped me to organize the materials and to pare down that initial manuscript to a more manageable size.

I then sent the manuscript off to Presidio Press. Bob Kane, the publisher of Presidio Press, called me and told me he thought I had a book but that it would need a great deal of work. He invited me and Margaret to come out to California, to stay at his home as his houseguests, and to work with him and his editor in chief, Adele Horwitz, to see if we could work the manuscript into publishable form.

I will always be grateful for that time spent staying with the Kanes and working at Presidio Press. I am also grateful for the patience Presidio Press has shown me, in my attempts to complete the book back here in Lincoln, under very hectic conditions.

Finally, I want to acknowledge the friendship of my aunt, Miss Ruth E. Berry, of Sioux City, Iowa. She spent many years studying and teaching American history. I hope this book will find an honored place on her shelves.

Prefatory Note

This book contains testimony from cases tried in Vietnam, 1968–69. In all instances but one, I have changed the names of my clients, for obvious reasons.

Parts of the Green Beret case are still classified secret; most of what is set forth here has been very recently declassified. Because the case received international attention, there would be no point in changing the names of those defendants. I hope and trust that nothing in this book will bring any of them embarrassment. They are all fine men.

The title, besides being an obvious echo of the "Ballad of the Green Berets," reflects one of the many angry letters written by concerned citizens to President Nixon while the Green Beret case was still in progress. This letter said, in part:

> Mr. President, I urge you to intervene in the murder charges against our eight great fighting men and give them what they really deserve: a medal for gallantry in action against an enemy. . . .

PART ONE

MOVING LITTLE

I had grown away from youth,
Shedding error where I could;
I was now essential wood,
Concentrating into truth:
What I did was small but good.

Orchard tree beside the road,
Bare to core, but living still!
Moving little was my skill.

— Yvor Winters,
  "A Dream Vision" from
  Two Old-Fashioned Songs

APRIL 26, 1969. WARRANT OFFICER VINCE SALARIO
*had been skimming the treetops, looking for his landing area.
His troops were at combat edge. Landings, especially secret
jungle landings, had become increasingly dangerous of late.
Somehow, in the least likely places, well-concealed and heavily
fortified enemy forces had been waiting to open fire. Salario
took a deep, sharp breath, and the ship touched down. Specialist
Angstrom was, as always, the first out, crouching low, running
beneath the whirling blade, his M-16 at ready. Then Corporal
Tiedebaum . . . It was then that the flash and the chatter of the
AK-47s became Salario's final reality. Slumped and bleeding,
his ship on fire and his men dead . . . his final thoughts must
have been "How did they know?"*

Salario is a composite character. But the question of how
Viet Cong or North Vietnamese forces managed to be ready for
our top-secret helicopter landings had vexed President Nixon
for months. The CIA had been humiliated by security leaks.
From an intelligence point of view, deaths like Salario's were
the supreme disaster. It indicated that in Cambodia (where the
Green Berets enjoyed secret CIA funding), NVA troops lay in
wait for top-secret intelligence missions. The Nixon administration was specifically denying that we were in Cambodia—
our officials were lying to the American people, as well as to our
South Vietnamese allies. And if the North Vietnamese knew of
our missions to Cambodia, our security problems were greater
than anybody had suspected.

This was the background for what was to become the most
perplexing and dangerous case of my career as a trial lawyer.
But it is impossible to explain my defense of those Special Forces
officers who were charged with executing the double agent
responsible for the compromise of certain intelligence and
counterintelligence networks, without some background as to
what I was doing in Vietnam from October 1968 until October
1969.

I tried lawsuits north near the DMZ, and south in the Delta;
I tried lawsuits in the angel wing of the Cambodian border, and

on the South China Sea. My courts-martial were wherever I was assigned, and I interviewed witnesses and wrote wills in all four corps areas of operations. I got shot at, and I fired back, but my perspective was that of a lawyer.

Any good lawyer lays his foundation; he knows how to offer evidence for limited purposes, and he is anxious to define the modesty of his enterprise. To say that the law is the limitation of my Vietnam vision is at once too narrow and too broad. I was also a soldier and a citizen—and there is no way one book could do justice to the subject, "the law in Vietnam." Reviewing testimony of cases I tried with numerous units—the 101st Airborne Division, the First Infantry Division, the First Cavalry Division, 5th Special Forces, and others. I find that my old cases draw what is, for me at least, a kind of experiential map of Vietnam.

A map has value only insofar as we can recognize its boundaries and understand its limitations. I write about law in Vietnam—about trying my courts-martial there—with a certain hesitancy. I approach my muse with less swagger than one might have expected; not from any notion of being coy, but because after nineteen years of trying lawsuits I am still not certain as to what the law is supposed to do, even under the simplest of circumstances.

And my cases! God, my cases. I remember being ordered to prosecute one of America's most decorated combat heroes on the charge that he sexually assaulted one of his men—never for a minute believing him guilty. And I think of defending two soldiers on a gang rape charge and losing my clients to Leavenworth but saving the marriage of one of the victims. I remember other cases, each significant and exotic in and of itself.

"Captain, I am not guilty. I have never committed a homosexual act in my life, and I did not touch that man." He looked me right in the eye.

I suppose it was a breach of protocol, that day in January 1969, when I sat at a table in the II Field Force Officers' Club bar, visiting with the soldier-defendant and his lawyer. They were both drinking Coca-Cola. I was drinking gin and tonic. I leaned back.

"I have my marching orders. The man claims it happened, and if the case isn't prosecuted, the judicial system will have stopped in midcycle; an officer's word will mean more than an enlisted man's. That's not the way it works."

I made a practical suggestion. "Look, convicted or acquitted, you're finished in the army. Resign from the service. I'll get you an honorable discharge. You go back a hero, the case disappears. Either that or we try it to a general court-martial. That's the best I can do for you." He took my advice and resigned. The solution to that problem had little to do with law, which does not always have much to do with justice.

The witness was sobbing, almost uncontrollably. My interpreter and I had been taking her statement in preparation for trial. There was no doubt in my mind that my two clients had gang-raped her, and there was no doubt in my mind that her testimony—along with other evidence—would surely convict them, so I already had a plea bargain struck. Still, it was my job to do the best I could for my men during the hearing on sentencing. Almost as an afterthought, I asked my interpreter: "See if there's anything I can do for her."

They talked together, quietly, intensely. "Sir, she says she wants a certificate of honorability. She says her husband won't sleep with her again until she has a document showing it wasn't her fault."

I had never heard of any such instrument, but I had with me a clerk-typist and an interpreter, and I composed a document in English, French, and Vietnamese, dated it, signed it with a flourish, and managed to attach some kind of ribbon and seal to it. She took the document, visibly grateful. I never saw her again. I had done what I could.

The captain and the Vietnamese lady had come within the sphere of the law, or rather within its gravity: the pull of the law's power. The problems were solved in ways having little to do with law as an abstract concept but having much to do with people, their injuries, wounds, fears, and loss of hope. I have heard complaints that a law degree is a license to steal; of course any professional license gives the "healer" commercial advantage over his "victim." But there is also the opportunity to dispense a little compassion, a little common sense—to help some poor bastard through the jungles and firefights of daily living. The law itself may be the solution, or part of the solution. It may also be at least part of the problem.

In the late fifteenth century the Renaissance was spreading in Western Europe. And in 1474, in Basel, a rooster came under the charge of having laid an egg. The human mind and spirit soared with magnificent cathedrals and paintings and the beginnings of great literature. The local prosecutor took the position that any rooster who laid an egg must be affiliated with the devil. The rooster was put to trial.

It is difficult not to sympathize with the earnest defense counsel, attempting as he did to persuade the court that the evidence against the rooster was not conclusive, that it was largely circumstantial, and that the rooster had not harmed anybody. From the available historical reports, it is impossible not to imagine the scrawny rooster sitting there in the courtroom, the defense lawyer pleading into the bored faces of the judges. With appropriate ceremony, the rooster was convicted and put to death. At about the time Shakespeare was born, ambitious prosecutors were bringing cases against animals, and against dead people, and against inanimate objects.

To state merely that the evolution of the law has been a little slow—that the law tends to lag behind the best thinkers of its time—would be an oversimplification. The law has always proceeded according to its own inscrutable pace—and no amount of scholarship or reform has ever made it any better than the people who administered it; and those of us who lawyered in Vietnam entered the country in ignorance. We did not know where we were, and we represented GIs, none of whom knew where they were. So we tried to work the approximate magic of the law in utter blindness, during a firestorm.

I found myself looking for clues and touchstones—anything to make myself less a tourist in uniform. Once in a small village near my base camp I saw people praying before a table covered with red cloth with four characters inscribed on it: *Bao Son Ky Hong.* I was told that this translates into "a good scent from a strange mountain": a celebration of Hoa Hao, an offshoot of Buddhism, with water and flowers offered in sacrifice. Elsewhere, a Buddhist village chief once admitted to me that he occasionally sought help from Taoist priests, with their magical rituals used to control the spirit world. "In the mid-July full moon forgive the wandering spirits." I learned of Trung Nguyen, Wandering Soul's Day, when the hungry spirits seek food left out for them. I witnessed Trung Thu, with moon cakes, lanterns designed like boats and fish, colorful parades with drums and cymbals.

I was painfully aware that the Vietnamese culture was rich and variegated beyond my comprehension; yet it seemed crucial that I try to gain and use insights into the Vietnamese people. If I could assimilate a part of their culture, I could do a better job of dealing with them and I would know how to question them as witnesses. And perhaps, during my daily life in Vietnam, I could end up doing more good than harm.

A great deal of fiction (some of it presented as fact) has created a peculiar orthodoxy about our forces engaged in the Vietnam War: the idea of a world without law, in which violent crime was ignored or even encouraged. This notion has been advanced in one of two ways: 1) by quoting anonymous sources, or 2) by reference to actual atrocity trials. The first method is a little weak as a truth-seeking device; the second method is self-contradictory, in that the prosecution of certain acts should make it clear that law did exist and was enforced in Vietnam. Clearly, there were times in the Vietnam War when killing was no crime. War includes killing, and by its very nature must give rise to circumstances that are morally and legally ambiguous.

One may ask hypothetically whether or not the execution of a dangerous double agent should be among those circumstances in which killing is not a crime. In the Green Beret case, we had to meet that issue squarely, and with very high stakes. But the fact that there were specific circumstances in which killing may not have been a crime does not mean that the law simply failed to function in Vietnam. The very eager acceptance of the notion of the Vietnam War as a place in which morals and law had entirely vanished is perhaps symptomatic of an age in which sloganeering has replaced thought in matters regarding war. In modern fiction the Vietnam soldier and veteran has replaced the proverbial butler as the prime suspect in crimes of violence.

During my year in Vietnam, 1968–69, cases were vigorously prosecuted and defended. I was chief defense counsel for II Field Force, which geographically corresponded with III Corps (north of the Delta and south of the Highlands) and which had general court-martial jurisdiction over eighty thousand men. My boss, Lt. Col. Robert W. Jones, knew I liked to travel, and knew I liked to try cases, and he was always willing to loan me out to divisions that needed me, anywhere in Vietnam. My clients knew they were standing trial, and some of them were sentenced to the federal penitentiary at Fort Leavenworth, Kansas. The law did exist and function in Vietnam, but it did so with certain very real limitations. Those limitations are more subtle and more fascinating than the fictional vacuum that has been so eagerly accepted as reality.

There are many cases that simply blur in my memory. There were acquittals for which no records were made, and it is impossible for me to reconstruct those cases. I remember some of my clients better than others, but to me, in retrospect, they all seem to be men who somehow survived the crisis of war and prosecution. Among them were those whose very humanity appeared to have been destroyed. Amid the ruins I sought gallantry where I could find it, and I pled for mercy where I could not.

The actions of a man at war must be judged in terms of who

that man was before he went to war; an isolated act of heroism or betrayal takes its meaning from the soldier's prior life history and the way in which that soldier, with that past, responds to a certain set of circumstances. Let there be no mistake: there is real heroism, and there is real cowardice. I have never suggested to any jury a purely mechanistic or deterministic theory of human behavior. But I did suggest, at court-martial after court-martial, that the court could not make its final judgment of the man and his actions until the jury had considered the man and his past. As to special circumstances—the members of the court were all serving in Vietnam at the time of the trials. They did not need to be informed or reminded that no word, thought, or deed in battle or under conditions of war has a precise peace-time parallel. We were all living on Mars, deceptively similar to Earth, and yet . . .

PART TWO

RUNNING, FRAGGING, AND RAGE

Shall I grapple with my destroyers
In the muscular poses of the museums?
But my destroyers avoid the museums.

> — *Wallace Stevens,*
> *"Like Decorations in a Nigger Cemetary"*

A DOZEN YEARS AGO, NEW YORK COCKTAIL PAR-
ties could be brought to life by the mere intonation of that
delicious word *fragging*. The thought of American soldiers killing one another with grenades was treated with exuberant good
humor. It was discussed as a significant act of war protest, a
little like carrying a picket sign. At the mere mention of the
phrase, the eyes did light up, the faces did glow like Halloween
pumpkins, the martinis did splash merrily in the glasses—fragging! The killing of officers by enlisted men was not as common
as the popular literature of the day had it. Fragmentation
grenades were one method of killing, and there were of course
many others. When American soldiers did die as the result of
American grenades, it was more often than not accidental. Still,
fragging had its aura of a kind of perverted glamor.

I

In late summer, 1969, I was sitting in a bar in Taiwan, drinking
with Lt. Col. Robert Jones and another senior military judge. We
sipped the rice beer, bragged about our trips to the aboriginal
villages and the Marble Gorge, the shrines we reached by crossing rope bridges high in the mountains, and of other shrines we
had found by following trails deep inside caves; but, inevitably,
the subject came back to The Law.

The bar was one of many in which, for fifteen dollars, the
customer "owned" a Chinese woman for twenty-four hours.
Although none of us had bought any of the girls—we all agreed
that prostitution was rape by billfold—we did enjoy going over
the little pink contract forms guaranteeing the women to be free
of health hazards and providing that the woman be returned by
the lessee in good condition, properly nourished and rested, fair
wear and tear excepted.

After we had exhausted our cumulative knowledge of the
law of contract (complicated law, we boozily agreed, only in
societies free enough to allow commercial choice), we began to
discuss famous cases: sometimes humorous, sometimes horrify-

ing, but all with an interesting legal twist. More beer came, and the military judge began to discuss an "amazing" case, with a factual basis that "you just won't believe." As he meandered through his narrative, I realized he was discussing one of my cases that had become a legend: the trial of Sergeant Arrigo, his background, his sentence.

I heard that case spoken of again and again throughout my stay in Vietnam. I still have a photograph of Sergeant Arrigo with his scout dog, King.

March 30, 1969, Phu Loi. The beer had made Arrigo first mellow, then morose. Although he could not have articulated it, the hours in which he was not on patrol with his dog had become unbearably empty. Perhaps his mind went back to his boyhood in Guam, where he had lived under a tree with his parents, hiding from the Japanese. Or to his wife who had refused to see him and had kept him from visiting his children, when last he had been in the World. He was alone, tossing an M-26 hand grenade from hand to hand. None of the other squad leaders were around to visit him. There had been a power failure, leaving the hooch and Arrigo in darkness, and alone. For no reason he could understand, Arrigo left the hooch, stood on the platoon road, pulled the pin and threw the grenade at the empty darkness. The silence was broken—first by the explosion of the fragmentation grenade, then by the scream of Arrigo's friend, Sergeant Wilson, who had been standing at a nearby urinal. Arrigo rushed Wilson to the dispensary, where Wilson died and Arrigo was given a sedative.

When I first met Arrigo at his scout dog platoon (assigned to that particular support battalion of the 3rd Brigade, 82nd Airborne Division), he took me to see his dog. Arrigo's English was not good, but he fully understood that he ran a risk of dishonorable discharge and three years confinement at hard labor. He was certain that if I could see him with his dog, I would know how to defend him, in a case in which he had already made a confession. He led me to understand that it was very important that he stay out in the field with King while awaiting trial. And I made him understand that since all we could do was plead guilty and try for a lenient sentence, he had better tell me everything—*everything*—about his life. It was difficult for him, but he agreed, and during the weeks before the trial, he would visit me from time to time at my office at the Plantation—the headquarters of II Field Force—located on Highway 1, about an hour northeast of Saigon. Or sometimes I would take the hot, dusty drive through countryside and small villages to his base at Phu Loi, to attend to other legal work, and to meet with him.

By the time we were before the sentencing court-martial, we were ready. Arrigo sat at attention that day in the II Field Force courtroom. The building had been struck by rocketfire and had machine gun holes in the roof from the previous Tet offensive; it was directly behind our front bunkers facing Highway 1. Across the street, a widows' village, a grouping of small shacks, occupied by a VC battalion just a few months before. The courtroom itself faced a "street"; the deliberation room was a screened porch in the back, where the court members could visit with one another and see our front bunkers and the highway. Arrigo, small, dark and muscular, was on edge; his neck muscles taut as brown ropes, his movement as stiff as a puppet on strings. He had just come from combat very different from the ordeal he was facing here. His remarkable testimony, I was certain, would humanize him to the court. A defense lawyer's primary job is to transform a problem person into a person with a problem before the court.

In response to my questions, he testified that he was one of eight children born to a family of poor Guamanians. When the Japanese invaded his island, he and his family moved to the jungle, where they lived under "a big shade tree." His father and older brother went out each day to hunt for food. One day the father was captured by the Japanese, and beaten, and eventually escaped from the Japanese, about six months before the Americans recaptured the island. The family moved from the tree to a cave, about twenty-five feet up a cliff over the ocean. They stayed there until the Americans came. After over four

years of living under a tree or in a cave, Arrigo knew the island
well and assisted the Americans in finding Japanese. The American forces set up a camp for the natives and opened a school.
Arrigo, who had completed second grade when the war broke
out, worked so that his sisters and younger brother could go to
school. His father had never fully recovered from the beatings
the Japanese had given him, so Arrigo was the main support for
his family, including his mother who had been ill for years.

The members of the court were listening intently. Arrigo
intrigued them; they were prepared to like him. He continued:
"When the Korean War broke out, I had a long talk with my
sister and I tell her I'm going to join the service; she tell me, 'No,
brother, you cannot join the service because you didn't go to
school. We can't send you to school, so we teach you.' . . . Every
night when I came home they set me down and they teach me.
In 1952, I passed. . . ."

He went on to testify about his first tour of combat duty in
Korea, about an attack by the Chinese. "We started firing and
firing. . . . We still couldn't hold them back, so we fixed bayo-
nets. . . . You didn't have to thrust your bayonet out when they
jump in. All you have to do is stick it out and you could catch
them. . . . Something hit me on the back of the neck. . . . I stayed
in the hospital for ninety days and now I'm back with the same
unit again. When my tour was almost completely up, I put in
for another six months' extension. . . ."

He told of his Guamanian bride, now living in Los Angeles,
of their children, of her leaving him because of his orders to go
to Vietnam:

> A: I went to Los Angeles and tried to see my wife and kids. I
>   call her up and she says, "No, you can't come and see the
>   kids." So I didn't argue, because I don't know much about
>   the law back there. I went to the police station and they
>   said, "What did your wife tell you?" I told them she said
>   not to come. He said, "You're supporting her?" I said, "Yes,
>   sir." He said, "Your best bet is not to go see her." So I didn't
>   argue. I went straight up on to Fort Benning and report in
>   there.

Q: You've been in the army how long?
A: Sixteen and a half years.
Q: You love the army, don't you?
A: Yes, sir.
Q: Showing you Defense Exhibit A, could you tell us, what is this picture?
A: That's me and my dog, King, sir.
Q: This is the dog that you went on patrols with, is that right?
A: Yes, sir.
Q: How much do you weigh?
A: 130 pounds, sir.
Q: And how much does your dog weigh?
A: 110 pounds, sir.

I called witnesses who had served with Arrigo in combat. I read letters from other men. My closing argument was lengthy, and I quote here only a small part of it:

> What do you think of the record of this man? Four years' education, this man grew up under a tree in a jungle in Guam while the Japanese occupied his island, a sick mother, a father captured by the Japanese. We're talking about a boy seven or eight years old, scouting around scrounging for food; a boy of absolutely no education whatever, by our standards, because I'm not talking about four years in an American school, I'm talking about four years in some school in Guam, as his entire educational background. And what has he done with that? He's come into the army, and this man is the best soldier he knows how to be. It's cost him a lot. It's cost him his wife; she won't live with him anymore because he would not attempt to get out of his orders to go to Vietnam. . . .

I remember Sergeant Arrigo standing there saluting the president of the court, ramrod stiff. His biceps quite literally quivered as his hand salute came up to his brow. The fingers of his left hand were extended and joined precisely as set forth in the field manual, his heels together; a man who was not trying to impress the court, but who was quite simply trying to be the very best soldier he could.

His sentence was this: he lost one stripe. He was reduced from staff sergeant E-5 to corporal E-4. He received no discharge, no confinement, no forfeiture, and no reprimand. He was back in the field the next day, soldiering with his beloved King. Somebody from *Overseas Weekly* met me later in the officers' club and congratulated me, called me a wizard. I liked Sergeant Arrigo, and I was glad for whatever I could do for him, but I did not feel much like a wizard. I could not get my mind off Sergeant Wilson, of the 37th Infantry Platoon. Did Wilson have a wife? Was his mother somewhere baking him cookies when Sergeant Arrigo threw a hand grenade and killed him? And how would they feel if they knew Arrigo had not lost a day's work over the incident? He was a good soldier and I liked him and I will forever remember his handshake as we parted. I wish him well, but I grieve for Wilson and his family. I remain more and more convinced that there should not have been a universe that contained both gun powder and alcohol.

My cases took me to places that were, by my standards at least, exotic: the Emperor's Study in the Citadel at Hue; the Saigon Zoo, with its famed white elephant, now sadly mottled; one tiny village where the chief (hunkering down under his thatched roof) told me that grave robbers often sought the head of a young girl, because it would bring them good luck. Another fragging case brought me to a part of Vietnam that was, to me, beautiful and exotic. Specialist Washington was at Fire Base Saint Barbara, an artillery camp in Tay Ninh Province. It was at the foot of the majestic and mysterious Nui Ba Den—a volcanic plug known as the Black Virgin Mountain.

I first saw the three-thousand-foot-high Black Virgin from my helicopter as we approached Saint Barbara. Long a part of the mythology of ancient Vietnam, it was intriguing with its lush tropical vegetation, and its many caves and tunnels. We controlled the top of the mountain and the area around the base, but the Cong owned the mountain itself. There is, I was told, a shrine somewhere on that mountain, commemorating a lovely Buddhist girl who died a martyr, then later appeared to a priest in a vision. From Firepoint Saint Barbara, outgoing artillery shells constantly banged away at whoever was hiding in the impenetrable vegetation.

Saint Barbara itself had a berm and bunker line. Outside the berm were three concentric rows of concertina wire with trip flares. There was, on three sides of the camp, a protective mine field between the first and second rows of wire. On the fourth side, of course, there was a road leading to Tay Ninh. The men lived in bunkers, and there was no alcohol or other form of entertainment anywhere on the fire base. Coming down in our helicopter, we could see the pockmarks and craters surrounding the fire support base, relics of Viet Cong rocket and mortar attacks. If Saint Barbara was flat and sandy and hot and loud, it was nevertheless squarely between two sublime points: the magnificent mountain, and the Cao Dai Temple in Tay Ninh. I had become familiar with the Cao Dai religion, and had heard of the temple, and was determined to make my visit.

The Temple was a stunning combination of pinks and whites, the white-robed worshippers kneeling on the floor. I thought of that religion especially once when my helicopter came low over a roof on which a huge blue all-seeing eye was painted—looking as startled as I felt by our encounter.

The heat. I recall clear, brutal heat from only two occasions: once was the first time I went to Saint Barbara; the other time was when I was defending a homicide (I forget the name of my client or the circumstances) that arose in a landing zone somewhere in the angel wing of the Cambodian border. Of the latter case I remember nothing except the polished boots standing in the morning memorial service—and the bunkers that were culvert halves, covered and surrounded by sand bags; the absence of any buildings you could stand in, or any water you could stand to drink; the Vietnamese wading in a pond just beyond the barbed wire.

In both places I remember most clearly (besides the heat and the noise) being able to set up my little lawyer shop and make myself available for the men, most of whom had never seen a lawyer in-country. The pure joy of lawyering! Chasing down a clerk-typist somewhere and serving the men who lined up.

Small problems to be handled as best I could: wills to be written, powers of attorney to be drawn up, and civilian attorneys back home to be dealt with—usually in a not very cordial letter declining to waive such rights as my client might have under the Soldiers and Sailors Civil Relief Act.

Problems of every kind, especially matrimonial problems. The war of the Dear John letters. A marriage can be a very frail thing, and it is not surprising when absence causes marriages to collapse. In past wars, however, there was usually a certain amount of hometown support for the man in uniform. And if a woman was lonesome, she could share in the public pride and affection for her husband, off fighting under the flag. There were pressures on wives in other wars—to be loyal to the man who, it was generally conceded, was involved in a difficult and necessary task.

In this war, wives were held to a lesser standard of loyalty than that due to a husband in a federal penitentiary. Adultery had become a mellow concept, betrayal without moral stigma. Marriages were collapsing, without the usual support structure that had helped them to withstand previous wars. I remember once when I was in Cam Ranh, I had occasion to visit a witness in the psychiatric ward of the 32nd Medical Depot. What I heard there had nothing to do with the horrors of combat. Screams of the horrors of betrayal. "That bitch! That bitch! Why won't she love me?" If there is a hell, the women who authored those letters will hear those screams.

The letters. Letters from wives. Letters—yes!—from the lovers of wives. Letters from civilian attorneys, complete with thoughtfully enclosed documents—sign here, soldier, and waive your rights. My clients were not unsettled by bad news. They were boys in a world of danger and sensory deprivation, aware that "the only confetti parade we'll get will be the shit people throw out their windows at us."

The wives and lovers who mailed off that psychic napalm intended no harm. People wanted to divorce and remarry, and the existence of a husband had become an inconvenience, which they hoped could be removed by a little reasonable correspondence. But the marriage that had become an inconvenience to the waiting wives and their home front heroes was often the entire emotional foundation for the boy who got the letter. I discovered that in addition to dispensing legal advice there was one other thing I could do: to give the most brutalized and emotionally crippled soldier a certain relief from his misery. To replace collapse with anger. A man began healing when instead of "my wife," he spoke of "that miserable bitch."

Right after I had landed at Saint Barbara, a First Cav slick* hovered in long enough to unload body bags and load up ammunition. My client, standing beside me, said: "Those twenty-seven-dollar Seiko watches from the PX still tickin' on the bodies. Ain't nothing but a body in that bag, but that watch is tickin'."

Reading through the record of that trial, I see quarrels between witnesses and lawyers as to red clusters which meant attack, white clusters which meant that the listening posts were coming in, etc. Pointless arguments arise during the course of any lengthy trial, and sometimes the heat or pure exhaustion had us litigating points of no consequence. There was always more work to do than could be done, too many cases to try, and the feeling of not having done enough. My fatigue was, at times, blinding. Then I would meet young riflemen, in the jungle, and I would know that my life was one of safety, ease and luxury. We lawyered seven days a week.

II

Christmas Eve, 1968
    A Red Cross girl who had been spending some spare time

---

*Utility helicopter for supply and service missions.

teaching English to teenagers in a Vietnamese orphanage had invited me to come and read *A Child's Christmas in Wales*. On the way back, my driver asked permission to stop briefly in the small village of Xa Tam Hiep to buy coal for a barbecue he and some of his friends were having that night. As we drove through the town, it occurred to me that this was the only time I had ever been away from the Plantation without my pistol and helmet. I felt festive and vulnerable, though my driver had his M-79 grenade launcher tucked under his seat. Twilight, the children playing in and around the dark narrow streets: *"Di di mau,"* they sang, running and skipping. Inside the tiny houses: lights that may have been Christmas candles, or lights before a family shrine, a general feeling of well-being on Christmas Eve. There had been rumors that we were going to get hit that night, but I could not bring myself to worry.

By happy coincidence, I had received my Christmas presents that day. My mother had sent me a very expensive wooden box of chocolates. On Christmas Day I hid the chocolates in my oversized briefcase and went to the USARV Installation Stockade at 10 Hall Road, Long Binh—also known as the Long Binh jail, or the LBJ. The sign over the gate: *We Welcome Command Failures*, flanked by the crossed pistols of the provost marshal. The ritual at the gate: remove pistol from holster, dry fire into red bucket, check in the cleared weapon. Then the briefcase inspection: flash the open valise at the bored specialist. He knew me well enough to mutter "Merry fucking Christmas" and nod me in, unaware of my contraband.

As always, I reported to Central Control, where I handed my bundle of name slips to the specialist who called off the names of my clients. They could hear their names over the loudspeaker system, and they came running, to form what one of them called "Captain Berry's Goon Platoon for Misfits and Dumbshits." Sam Gomez was usually the leader of my "goon platoon." He marched in front and carried my briefcase. I always examined and cross-examined each in the presence of the others and made them criticize one another. They were rooting for each other, and their sense of comradeship made the waiting less horrible.

Sometimes we met in the mess hall, a large dining area, and high on the walls the flags of each of the fifty states. A dark summer camp humor: I would imagine tables of pink-cheeked prisoners, singing for their home states, "Indiana, our Indiana . . ." On this Christmas Day we found a small private conference room with a table and enough chairs. I opened my briefcase and brought out the candy. We ate it, both in honor of Christmas and to celebrate one client's birthday.

We talked about our family Christmases, what we did at home, and then, before I left, I concluded with this statement: "I wish you a Merry Christmas. I promise each of you that your next year's Christmas will be merrier than this one was. I cannot promise you a Happy New Year, but I can promise you a happier New Year than you had this past year." We shook hands, concluding our small ceremony to consecrate the holiday.

I liked my clients. In any busy law practice, a lawyer is bound to represent a number of people whom he does not like, but I liked these men. I see them clearly in my mind's eye, and I remember their postures, facial expressions, and tones of voices, things I had hoped I could use to obtain mercy for them. God knows, I wasn't relying on the law.

My favorite client at that Christmas party was Jay Kraus. A Methodist boy, converted to Buddhism, he had asked me to bring him a small ivory Buddha on a chain. At the time, it seemed an appropriate Christmas present. In 1967, he had twice received nonjudicial punishment under Article 15, the first for "failure to repair" and the second for a short absence without leave the day before his scheduled departure back from Vietnam to America.

Kraus was a tough kid, but apparently not tough enough to be willing to go back to the States after he finished his first tour in Vietnam. I know of one captain who missed a flight home, simply delaying the terrifying moment of return, a leper from

Mars. The more skeptical among us understood that we had all
undergone too much psychic damage to be ready for the abuse,
or at least indifference, awaiting us back home. A pint of gin
bloused into the jungle fatigues for the flight home: holy water
against the terror of return.

At the USARV Installation Stockade, Kraus was genuinely
feared, though he was not waiting trial for any crimes of violence, but rather was charged with having been Absent Without
Leave. When he was apprehended, he was found to have some
LSD, some marijuana, and an unauthorized sidearm in his possession, and of course, his contraband led to additional charges.
He was 5 feet 8 inches, and he could not have weighed over 145
pounds. His hair, which was worn short, had been dyed black
so he could pass for Vietnamese. On one arm he had tattooed
the Vietnamese word for death and on the other, the Chinese
symbol for long life. He was known in the stockade as "Mr.
Evil." He was chillingly courteous.

In the military, if the defendant pleads guilty, thereby saving the government the time and expense of trying a case, that
in itself is a matter of extenuation and mitigation for sentencing
purposes. A plea bargain may involve an agreement limiting the
maximum possible sentence. So, in cases that were clear losers,
the strategy was to strike the plea bargain, put on evidence for
sentencing purposes, then to "beat the deal," to get a better
sentence from the court than had been negotiated with the
appointing authority.

"Talk to me! Tell me about yourselves!" I tried to develop a
rapport that would withstand the alienating conditions of the
courtroom. Later I would use their combat experience to humanize them to the court, make the court think, "This good
combat soldier is in trouble. What can I do to help?"

The members of the court-martial were never there because
they wanted to be; they were there because somebody had cut
orders on them. Their own missions were being neglected so
they could sit on a jury. Each of the officers on the court had, at
some point, taken a course in military law and was familiar
with the Manual for Courts-Martial. Each had administered

punishment under Article 15, for minor offenses. Each court was, in short, a group of part-time magistrates and justices of the peace, gathered into a big time jury.

I had to show the court that Kraus had been a good point man. I wanted him to tell them the same stories he told me: how the presence of Viet Cong was often simply sensed intuitively and instinctively; how their booby traps were marked by signs such as three palm leaves tied together; of the *Tu Dia* sign with its skull and crossbones, alerting other VC and attracting Americans; of other markings, signals and clues. I wanted him to discuss the varieties of traps, especially the spiked trench with sharpened bamboo sticks in the bottom; the adjoining trench tunnel with the enemy soldier waiting to finish off whatever the spikes had not done. These were all aspects of being a point man for the Redcatchers of the 199th Brigade. They were matters the court members could appreciate, and their esteem for a good soldier could only help the defense.

Kraus made the decision not to testify about those details, telling me, "So, I walked point. Either they know what that means or they don't. That's all there is to it and I won't testify about it further."

We had made our plea-bargaining deal with the appointing authority. It remained only for Kraus to plead quilty, and for us to see if we could get a sentence lower than maximum punishment the appointing authority had agreed upon. Kraus limped toward the witness stand, one foot in a heavy bandage, and sat, contained and still, as if listening for danger in the distance as I questioned him:

Q:　And would you tell us when you first came to Vietnam?
A:　In May '66, sir.
Q:　Was that voluntarily?
A:　Yes, sir.
Q:　And what was your job then?
A:　I was in the 1st Cavalry Division as a point man in a line unit.
Q:　And at this time where were you physically in Vietnam?

A: I was in the Tuy Hoa area, Bong Son, along the Laotian border, and I was also in the 1st Cav at Pleiku.

Q: Did you receive the Combat Infantryman's Badge at this time?

A: Yes, sir.

Q: And what were your duties as a point man with a line unit with the 1st Cav at this time?

A: As point man, sir, it was my job to clear the area visually as best I could, or physically, and make sure the area was safe for the individuals following behind me.

Q: Did you enjoy your work?

A: Yes, sir.

Q: And what was the next job you held after that?

A: I went to the Aviation in Bien Hoa, which is the 334th Armed Helicopter Company. I was a gunner on a gunship.

Q: Did you fly any missions?

A: A little over a hundred.

Q: And what did you then do?

A: From there I was sent to the U.S.

Q: And what did you do once you were sent to the U.S.?

A: I went through all procedures that I could find to be returned to Vietnam. I returned with 5th Battalion, 12th Infantry, which was then being assigned to the 199th.

Q: What was your job with the 5th, 12th and 199th?

A: E Company recon, sir. I was a point man for the recon platoon.

Q: Did you like the job?

A: Yes, sir.

Q: Did you ever request to be transferred into any other unit or any other kind of job?

A: Yes, sir, one time I submitted a 1049 form to be transferred to MACV Headquarters, to be reassigned to a CID unit or an RFPF platoon.

Q: Why did you want to work with the RFPF platoon?

This question had the court members joining in. Each of them, by facial expression, seemed to be saying, "Yes, tell us why on earth anyone would want to be assigned to them."

A: Because due to the length of time I've spent in this country, sir, I've come to know the people quite well—the language and the customs—and I felt I could be of some benefit.

Q: Pfc. Kraus, the charges against you are clearly serious, and I want the court to know why it was, and the circumstances that you left your unit when you did.

A: I can explain it, sir.

Q: Would you please?

A: At the time that I was sent out of the country from the aviation unit at Bien Hoa, I had applied to be married to a Vietnamese national, which was refused. I tried to go through other legal procedures to get this done. I was again refused. They cut my orders one morning, gave me clearance papers, and I was sent to the U.S., and then I was sent to the Long Binh post here as a replacement with the Armed Guard. After I returned I made several attempts, going through my platoon leader and my platoon sergeant, trying to get a 3-day pass, leave or any other type of legal action I could, to go to the Saigon area to find her, which was also refused.

Q: And did you have any additional information regarding your fiancée which made you want to see her more?

A: I was aware of the fact that she had my child. I couldn't locate either one at the time.

Q: And when you left, were you looking for her and your child?

A: I was, sir.

The court liked him, and I rushed him through his testimony. His platoon leader testified that he wanted him back:

Q: And I'd like you to tell us in your own words what you can about the nature and quality of his duties as your point man?

A: Well, sir, he told us that he wanted to be point man from the standpoint it would give him a feeling of accomplishment. . . . He would hold up the patrol on any movement if he decided that any old bunkers, new bunkers—anything he found suspicious—hold up the patrol, go ahead check it out. If it was a fighting position of some type, he automatically just went ahead and put a grenade into it and brought the rest of the patrol up.

The court was sympathetic, as were the staff judge advocate and the commanding officer. Kraus was sent back out to
the field with no punishment. I was smug and self-satisfied,
never guessing that Kraus was turning invisible corners, walking point through the mine field of his own inner self.

*Kraus knew he was tired. He could not have known that
later he would be diagnosed as borderline schizophrenic. He
had been having visual hallucinations for some time. He thought
they might be LSD flashbacks. Once, on a raft, he and his squad
came under VC fire. A Russian-made rocket-propelled grenade
exploded directly in front of his face, killing the man to his right
and wounding three men to his left. Since then, he began to see
what he called "mental pictures," and for some time he had felt
himself under constant attack; any movement of any kind
seemed to him to be an attack. On April 7, 1969, he came into
An-Lac Village, Hamlet #4, Binh Chan. Earlier that day, he had
discovered a series of fresh trenches. There he had found some
Cambodian money, some documents, and a "four pound
grenade set up as a booby trap." He had disarmed the huge
grenade, gathered the documents, turned the documents in to
his CP, checked the claymore mines for the night, and then had
gone to a Vietnamese house for Coca-Cola. He was nervous. He
heard his Vietnamese name, Tuen, called. He went to the door,
was jostled, and fired.*

The next time I saw Kraus, he was facing these new charges:

> Specification: In that Private E-1 Jay R. Kraus, U.S. Army, Com-
> pany E, 5th Battalion, 12th Infantry, 199th Infantry Brigade
> (Separate) (Light), did, at An-Lac Village, Hamlet #4, Binh
> Chan, Republic of Vietnam, on or about 7 April 1969, commit
> an assault upon Thi Chin Nguyen by shooting her in the left arm
> with a pistol and did thereby intentionally inflict grievous bodily
> harm to her, to wit: a fracture of the left humerus.

The case had arisen near the Fishnet, an abandoned fishnet
factory on the banks of a river. It had been taken over as the forward area of the 199th Light Infantry brigade. The area was

surrounded by Viet Cong villages. It was not uncommon for explosives to come floating down the river, and I once came under fire in a small neighboring village. Another time, nearby, I had presented myself to a village chief, to ask his permission to enter his village with my interpreter to meet with witnesses. He was more than hospitable, giving me my first and only taste of what I believe was absinthe.

I had gone to An-Lac to investigate Kraus's case and had met the prosecution witnesses and had liked them. When we finally began our trial, the first witness was Nguyen Thi Lieu, a fragile, darkly attractive girl from the village of An-Lac.

She identified herself as coming from the Binh Chan District, Gia Dinh Province. She properly identified Kraus, giving him a slight, apologetic smile as she did so. The interpreter was a tiger scout who had gone with me on many a mission. Mr. Xuan was clearly cheering for the defense. I suppose if a person has to undergo the ordeal of conducting cross-examination through an interpreter, it is good to have a friend doing the interpreting.

Having properly identified herself, and the defendant, and having had her memory directed to April 7, 1969, the witness continued:

> On that night I saw that one GI sat with one girl on table and drink coke and after that about five minutes a Vietnamese man came in the house and this GI invite him for a drink of coke. After that have one man named Xuan come in the house and ask GI for coke but GI say no. After that he ask for cigarette and he get one cigarette and he sit down and talk to the lady and after that have one man come in and this girl sit on his knee say this man outside the house and seem very happy and run out of the house and talk to this man and after that other people went out of the house and that GI went out and shoot.

Her testimony was lengthy and thorough. As I began my cross-examination, I took out a photograph of the house, with a transparent cover, and gave her a grease pencil. It had been difficult to get a good picture of the house because of the way in which it was surrounded by thick vegetation. The house itself was made of poles and leaves, but with a tin roof and sandbags piled up beside the bedroom. She made a number of marks, identified where everything was, and drew lines showing the action.

> Q: Now when you were coming in the doorway that the GI was standing in right before the pistol went bang, do you remember if you touched him in any way? Did he brush against you or touch you in any way?
> A: Sir, when I went in the house, GI stand right in the door and he touch me by his arm.
> Q: So you touched the GI's arm at about the time the gun went bang?
> A: Yes, sir.
> Q: Do you think that the GI shot your aunt on purpose?
> A: No, I don't know, sir.

After the prosecution rested, I called Kraus, to tell me about the day it all happened, beginning with his exploration of a series of fresh trenches.

> Q: And what else did you find?
> A: I found about the largest grenade I've ever seen in Vietnam. It weighed anything from two and a half to four pounds and it was set up as a booby trap.
> Q: What did you do?
> A: I disarmed it.
> Q: Did you find any documents?
> A: Yes, numerous documents which I believed to be squad leader's identification papers.
> Q: Did you sort these documents?
> A: Yes, sir, they were a little mixed up with a lot of propaganda leaflets dropped by Americans. The people in my platoon didn't know the difference.

I stopped to glance at one of the court members, an officer whose assignment was in "psy-ops," broadcasting and dropping leaflets, night after night; "professional litterbugs," he and his unit called themselves.

A: Yes, sir. We were picked up and went back to the bridge.

Q: Now, I want you to describe your actions of that evening.

A: After I got off the patrol, I went back and went immediately to the CP to turn over the items we had picked up and give any reports that we had. I left most of it up to Sgt. Porter who was our platoon sergeant at the time. I went from there back to my bunker. The first thing I did was check the claymores because it was about to get dark, about an hour before dark. I checked everything that it was my responsibility to check including the people to set up on guard. I discovered that I pulled guard more or less early in the morning, so I told everybody that I would try to get some sleep, went inside the bunker.

Q: Were you able to sleep?

A: No, sir.

Q: Why was that?

A: Just nervous.

Q: What did you then do?

A: At that point I just got up out of the bunker and I walked across the road to this house where I knew some Vietnamese had cokes that they sell.

Q: What happened after you entered the house?

A: I walked into the house. I didn't just walk in because I was rather doubtful as to what the status of the place was. I didn't know if it was a Vietnamese household or business or anything like that so I hesitated outside for a few minutes.

Q: You stated, did you not, that they sold cokes there?

A: Yes, sir. I was asked to go inside and they asked me what I wanted. I asked them if I could buy a coke. Then they consented, got a glass, put some ice in it. I paid for it and I was sitting on a chair and a female-type Vietnamese came in and made it a point to start a conversation with me.

The court was composed of men whose experience enabled them to hear Kraus's testimony with a very strong sense of place. They leaned forward, and I could tell they were hearing what he had heard and feeling what he had felt. This is testi-

mony at its best. It is a kind of magic that arises between a prepared witness and an attentive jury. The lawyer's job is to draw
the jury into his client's private world of perceptions so they can
experience the incident along with him. The magic was working
here.

Q: What was your reaction to being in this situation?
A: Frankly, I was worried, sir.

Q: Why were you worried?
A: Because it was an ideal setup.

Q: When you say ideal setup, what do you mean?
A: I hadn't had it constantly in my mind for the past two or
    three days, but it was always in the back of my mind that
    somebody was going to get me and all of a sudden I find
    one individual very friendly whose voice changes to one of
    fear and removes themselves from the room, then every-
    body just—out the door and I'm left there alone.

Q: Okay, what happened then, if anything?
A: About the same time I heard people moving towards the
    door, moving toward the house itself down the path from
    the road. I heard the noise which kept getting increasingly
    louder and finally I heard the girl, a voice call me, call for
    me three times. She called me in Vietnamese.

Q: Do you have a Vietnamese name?
A: Yes, sir.

Q: What is your Vietnamese name?
A: Tuen.

Q: She called, "Tuen"?
A: That's right.

Q: And how did you interpret this?
A: She sounded to me like she might have some kind of prob-
    lem out there. I wasn't sure what was going on. I got up
    from the chair I was sitting in and started toward the door.

Q: As you were moving toward the door, what if anything did
    you do with your weapon?
A: I just figured I'd been here too long to get knocked off by a
    bunch of silly PFs. The reason I did that was from my own
    judgment because I figured it would not be detrimental to
    anyone to have a loaded weapon because I thought that I
    was in a bad situation.

The court liked that. The idea of having "been here too long" to be killed as a result of incompetence on the part of our allies was a universal concern. There was nobody who had not felt that and who could not sympathize with it. The court members by now were nodding along with Kraus. The president of the court actually had his fist clenched, and I half expected him to start leading a cheer on Kraus's behalf. I moved on quickly.

Q: Okay, what did you then do?
A: I got up from the stool, chambering a round in the weapon at the same time, and moved towards the doorway. Just at the time my body entered the doorway I bumped into the little girl. She was coming in the door.
Q: And had you seen her coming out of the dark at this time?
A: No, sir. She came more or less off at an angle. I couldn't see her from inside the house. I could have seen her if I had been standing in the doorway.
Q: What happened when you bumped into one another?
A: She kind of scrunched her shoulders all up and scrunched up like she was getting between me and the doorjam inside and for no apparent reason she just did a real quick spin right where she was and bumped against my arm.
Q: What happened then?
A: My weapon discharged.
Q: Did you see where the weapon discharged?
A: Yes, sir. I did.
Q: Who was hurt?
A: A woman known as Thi Chin.
Q: Okay, what did you then do?
A: I didn't know what to do really. The first thing I thought I'd better do is clear the weapon but upon seeing that immediately thereafter the weapon went off I saw that the woman was hurt. The first thing that entered my head was somebody was going to need a doctor or a bandage.

The case ran on, and Kraus testified well. I had been watching him closely, and watching members of the court. They were running with him; there was no doubt of that. It crossed my mind that this was an acquittal, and that the court would agree that the shooting had been an accident.

I happened to glance over at the court reporter, talking into his machine. I was startled to discover that the red light was off. I asked the judge if I could approach the bench. The military judge was surprised that I interrupted myself, but he invited me to the bench. I told the court that the recording machine was not working; testimony had been lost, and the trial was no good. It was late in the evening, and I moved for mistrial. The judge granted my motion, and we went our separate ways. The officers on the court returned to their units, and the prosecutor, Capt. Frank Dicello, and I wandered over to the officers' club for a gin and tonic.

A few days later, I learned that Kraus would receive an administrative discharge, and that he could be processed out of the army if he would (in the presence of his lawyer) sign a waiver of his rights to a hearing. The administrative discharge he would receive was not one we had earlier requested (on the advice of a stockade mental health specialist), but it was good for Kraus. He would take an undesirable discharge for unfitness but that did not matter; he wanted out. About a week later, I came into my office. Kraus was sitting there smiling. "What are you doing?" I asked. "Oh hell, I'm just sitting here, waiting for the waiver man." I witnessed his signature on the waiver form, relieved him of an unauthorized pistol he was carrying in his field jacket (similar to the one he had had in possession when he was first arrested?), disassembled it, and threw the pieces into a toilet in a nearby outhouse. (What should I have done? Pressed charges against him?) I shook his hand. He went home to new waivers, a new life.

III

Saigon.

The city gleamed with the hard clear energy of survival; the fortunate soldier glanced off the blinding surface and went his way. Those who broke through the surface stayed forever.

Drugs, romance, adventure—a city where it was common to wear a sidearm; a town filled with good restaurants and criminal organizations from throughout the Far East, anxious to hire the American deserter with his inevitable French I.D. Sometimes I think of them—the thousands of deserters who took up life in Saigon. What became of them after our retreat and surrender? Where are they now, and what are they doing? It would be romantic to believe they were real survivors—people who had learned to live by their wits, and could survive anything— and are now living as soldiers of fortune or as happy husbands somewhere in the Orient. Perhaps they never had to leave Saigon. But for Western man the levantine acid of time works with a lethal swiftness.

Bill O'Brien was confused. After his months as a medical corpsman with the 101st Airborne, he had come to Saigon and had fallen in love. . . . He had moved in with his woman, and she had needed more and more money, so he went to a black-market money exchange, the home of a woman named Pham Thi Sinh. Maybe it was the old epilepsy, or the drugs, but, there in her bedroom, he stabbed her, and stabbed her.

O'Brien was a tall, pale youth with a kind of altar boy handsomeness to him. As a child he had been the good boy who not only survived his parents' divorce, but who had worked hard at staying close to both parents. He had concealed his history of epilepsy to get into the army, where he received the Combat Paratrooper Badge, the badge of a medical assistant, and other decorations.

O'Brien was with the 101st Airborne Division and had extended his tour in Vietnam so that one of his brothers would not have to come to war. He had been a perfect soldier in Vietnam, without leave, and without R & R for almost eleven months. I have a photograph of him and his blonde high school sweetheart at their prom: he in a white jacket and black tie, she looking up adoringly, the top of her head coming just to his shoulder. The charges were as follows:

Charge I: Violation of the Uniform Code of Military Justice, Article 118

Specification 1: In that Private First Class William F. O'Brien, Headquarters and Headquarters Company, 326th Medical Battalion, 101st Airborne Division, APO San Francisco 96383, did, at 220/150/3 Truong Minh Giang, Saigon, Republic of Vietnam, on or about 2 December 1968, while perpetrating a robbery, murder Pham Thi Sinh by means of stabbing her with a knife.

Specification 2: In that Private First Class William F. O'Brien, Headquarters and Headquarters Company, 326th Medical Battalion, 101st Airborne Division, APO San Francisco 96383, did, at 220/150/3 Truong Minh Giang, Saigon, Republic of Vietnam, on or about 2 December 1968, while perpetrating a robbery, murder Gia Bui Thi by shooting her with a pistol.

Charge II: Violation of the Uniform Code of Military Justice, Article 122: In that Private First Class William F. O'Brien, Headquarters and Headquarters Company, 326th Medical Battalion, 101st Airborne Division, APO San Francisco 96383, did, at 220/150/3 Truong Minh Giang, Saigon, Republic of Vietnam, on or about 2 December 1968, by means of force and violence steal from the person of Pham Thi Sinh, against her will, military payment certificates of a value of about $3,700, the property of Pham Thi Sinh.

It has always been my compulsion to investigate my cases personally; to go *to the scene*, whether in the jungle, or the criminal subcultures of Saigon, or elsewhere. My investigation of O'Brien's case took me to the seedy offices of the Criminal Investigation (CID) in Saigon; to the Vietnamese jail where he had been confined. I visited the house where the killing took place; I was present when O'Brien was identified by Vietnamese witnesses in a lineup; I went with him to the hospital for his neurological tests; once, interviewing character witnesses out in the field, I became involved in a brief, terrifying firefight.

O'Brien spent most of his pretrial time with the 101st Airborne Division up near the DMZ. He was confined part of the time at the Third Marine Amphibious Force Brig at Da Nang. When I was trying to put together a psychiatric defense, I had him moved to confinement at the USARV Installation Stockade at Long Binh. One day, I had him with me at my office at the Plantation. He was seated, still in irons, at my desk as I went over some pretrial motions with him.

At II Field Force we did without the luxuries of Saigon or Long Binh, but we had decent offices. A quonset hut divided into small carrels, an overhead fan and a water cooler filled with yellowish water that tasted (of course) of iodine and chemicals. A small banana tree by the front door, a bunker directly south of us, and an outhouse right behind the office. A good, secure building with a few machine gun holes left over from last Tet. It was a fine office, especially compared to the tents and bunkers where I did most of my lawyering. My driver was in the process of removing O'Brien's irons, and I had my feet up on the desk, trying to put O'Brien at ease, so we could get down to work.

The sergeant major rapped on the walls of my carrel. "It's urgent, Captain," he said. That could mean anything, and I walked out to the front of the office, wondering if I should have brought my steel helmet and .45 pistol from my desk. "It's O'Brien's twin brother, Captain. Chopper door gunner—just bought the farm."

O'Brien was young, frail in his way. In combat, in his life at Saigon, and in the Vietnamese jail, he had taken all he could take. Now, I had to tell him his twin brother was dead. I took my driver aside: "Bender, take O'Brien down to the EM mess. Take the irons off him, and stay with him. Get him some good chow and a beer, then take him back to your hooch and let him lie down for a few minutes." So they walked off together, O'Brien to eat as a free man for the first time in months. Bender to sit next to him, his hand occasionally slipping down to his holstered .45 pistol.

Pathetic, vulnerable, the way O'Brien went off unquestioning, not knowing that I was giving him gentle treatment before administering the coup de grace. I knew the case was over. The fight went out of him as I knew it would. He told me to make whatever kind of plea bargain I could, he just wanted to plead guilty and get the case over with. But it struck me that there were still a few things I could do for him.

In the military, the same court that finds a man guilty fixes his sentence. And there is always evidence that defense counsel may offer in "mitigation and extenuation" for sentencing purposes.

I decided to visit O'Brien's unit, to find as many of his buddies as I could, and to get them to testify on his behalf. Additionally, I sought out the addresses of his friends who had gone home, and I wrote to them, asking them for letters that could be read for sentencing. Of course, I wrote to his family, asking them to send me letters, too.

We finally assembled at Camp Eagle, in a courtroom of sorts, where it was at least one hundred degrees. We selected our court and began the proceedings. I knew that I would be talking for at least nine hours in that heat—I also knew that the members of the court would want to get out of there and back to the war. O'Brien was going to have one day to enter his plea and to be sentenced—I was going to do my best to make that one day count.

I filed a flurry of motions to dismiss, all of which the military judge overruled. I had made a good record for whoever eventually saw this case on appeal. I then advised the law officer (still out of the hearing of the officers who would compose the court) that my client was going to be pleading guilty to murder.* The law officer wanted to make certain that the defendant's guilty plea was prudently and providently taken. O'Brien was sworn and took the stand. His face had the same dull, defeated expression as it had the moment I told him of his brother's death. He slumped forward in his chair, his hands hanging limp. His demeanor was that of a beaten man attempting courtesy:

*The law officer was, of course, a legally trained member of the Judge Advocate General's Corps. Although the title "law officer" was changed to "military judge" in late 1969 or early 1970, his function remained the same: to make rulings as to law, and to instruct the "jury."

LAW OFFICER: Now you have a legal and moral right to plead not guilty, and put the burden on the prosecution of proving you guilty beyond a reasonable doubt. If he failed to do so, and you pleaded not guilty, the court could not find you guilty.

There's nothing wrong with pleading not guilty, even though you know you are guilty, even though you feel you are guilty. It's not a sin, it's not a lie to stand up in court and say, I plead not guilty, even though you know you are guilty, even though you feel you are guilty. What you are doing in that event is availing yourself of the presumption of innocence and you are doing nothing but forcing the government to prove you guilty beyond a reasonable doubt.

Under our system of law, the accused does not have to prove he is innocent. The burden is on the prosecution to prove him guilty and if the government cannot meet its burden, then the court can't find you guilty of the offense charged.

Now every offense in our criminal law has parts to it; these parts are called elements by lawyers and by judges. When you plead guilty, you would admit to every one of those elements or parts. If you plead not guilty, the government would have to prove every one of those elements or parts beyond a reasonable doubt.

Do you understand that?

ACCUSED: Yes, sir, I do.

My client was there to lie down and die.

The day moved on apace:

CAPTAIN BERRY: Now, sir, Defense exhibit 4 is a psychiatric report taken by Capt. John K. Imahara at USARV Installation Stockade.

Defense Exhibit 5 is a neurological examination taken by Dr. Ketch who is the neurologist at the 93d Evac Hospital.

Defense Exhibit 6 is a statement as to the accused's epileptic history as stated by his doctor, Stanford, who is his family physician.

There is no issue as to the accused's sanity because the psychiatrists and psychologists have found that he is sane and was legally sane at the time of the offense.

He is an epileptic and the neurologist has found that he did not perform the act in question while under psychomotor or other epileptic seizure. The neurologist provided us no defense.

The issue as to the accused's sanity is therefore resolved insofar as the previous provident plea; however, the accused will testify under oath during his extenuation and mitigation, that the moment of the stabbing he was under the influence of marijuana.

This is, of course, discussed by Capt. Imahara and by the neurologist, both whom found that it did not impair his ability to tell right from wrong or to adhere to the right. It will be solely for the purpose of showing mitigation. Also as Capt. Imahara discusses in his psychological report, the accused was having mild hallucinations at the time. However, as Capt. Imahara stated under the circumstances the accused was sane; the hallucinations had to do with the supposed presence of policemen coming on the scene and so forth. Capt. Imahara thinks that this was a reasonable feeling for him to have under the circumstances.

Many relatives will write that they do not believe that the accused was capable of an act of violence if he were himself. Now this is being brought into the court only to show the kind of feelings the accused invokes in other people. It's not going to go to the issue of the accused's sanity at the time.

In short, sir, as you saw from the stipulation, the accused grabbed the woman by the throat when he heard a shot downstairs. His buddy yelled "kill her, kill her" and he stabbed her 4 times. This entire incident is adequately bizarre, especially since the accused has no previous convictions.

Perhaps somebody, somewhere, would show this boy some mercy. I wanted it all in the record.

We were still out of the hearing of the "jury." The judge asked O'Brien what had happened.

ACCUSED: Well, we went into the house and we went upstairs. This mama-san worked in the black market—money orders, things like that. We went upstairs where she kept all her money and Baker followed me up the stairs. Wilson was going to stay downstairs and tie up the maid.

We got upstairs, and we were seated at the desk and we were

facing the stairway, and she was sitting between me and the stairway.

Well, all of a sudden we started hearing these screams from downstairs and I could see down there where Wilson was at and Wilson was beating this mama-san on the head with his .45 caliber pistol. Well it seemed like that her screams were attracting police, that they were all coming in the house and this mama-san from upstairs, she jumped up from her desk and started running for the stairs. At that time I grabbed her around the neck, sir.

JUDGE: And you knew you were grabbing her around the neck at the time?

ACCUSED: Yes, sir, I did, to keep her from screaming and well, I held her and she went limp, and I lowered her to the floor, her head hit the railing . . .

JUDGE: Banister?

ACCUSED: Banister and at the same moment, Wilson fired a shot downstairs and I looked down and I saw that he shot the mama-san through the head with the .45 to stop her screaming and it seemed like, well when this mama-san fell to the floor and hit her head, it seemed like that the police were downstairs and they were all over, around me and Baker was yelling "stab her, stab her" and like that . . .

JUDGE: And when he said "stab her, stab her" did you understand what he said?

ACCUSED: Yes, sir, I did.

In any criminal case, the problem of uncharged misconduct will arise. Suppose a defendant is charged with crime A, but, in order to prove crime A, the prosecution has to also prove crimes X, Y and Z. Military judges (or law officers as they used to be called) are much more scrupulous than civilian courts in excluding uncharged misconduct. Part of our out-of-court hearing had to do with that matter:

CAPTAIN BERRY: The accused is going to show by his testimony under oath, that the time he went AWOL, he intended to take a little French leave and come back. When he got up to Saigon, he got involved with a woman. Now this is of course un-charged misconduct to start with, relationship with the Vietna-mese woman, but we will show that the Vietnamese woman con-vinced him not to return when he wanted to return and she con-vinced him to go after money. That she constantly needed more money and she further was an individual who kept drugs and dope in the house. Now this will be shown in light of a young man who previously had no record, he got in with an evil woman. I think that it is necessary to show all this to the court to understand the precise circumstances in this case. This man . . . had an excellent record, until he found himself in this position.

The judge, prosecutor and I agreed upon our procedure. The court was called back in, and away we went. His sister had written me this letter, which I read to the entire court:

. . . I'm Pfc. William O'Brien's sister and I'm willing to help him out in any way I can. Bill's been a real swell brother ever since we were small children, he always tried to teach me right from wrong. I'm sorry I really don't know what to write except that I love him a lot and pray to God that he comes home safe and sound. In my opinion I don't think Bill would commit a crime, because he just isn't that kind of a boy. I could remember when we were younger and all still at home, on Sunday morning we would all walk to church together. In the summer we would all go swimming and go on picnics and Bill never got into any trou-ble. What I mean is, he had a few fights with other guys but nothing serious; it was mostly just to see who was stronger. When I heard the news about Bill being in jail, I couldn't believe what I was hearing because I expected him home in December. If there's anything I can do, please let me know. I'd do anything in my power that I can do. He's the only big brother I have left. My parents along with all the rest of us received word that my other brother, Specialist Four Ronald O'Brien was killed in action in Vietnam and that's why Bill's the only big brother that I have left. So please send him home safely.

The letters held a certain fascination for me. I did not want to lose the court's interest, but I wanted (for reasons that had nothing to do with the lawsuit) to bring the spark of life back into O'Brien's eyes—reading these letters aloud, showing him how others cared about him, could, I thought, begin the healing process that might eventually put the spring back in this young man's step.

I continued with a letter from his mother:

> To Whom It May Concern: I am writing you concerning Pfc. William F. O'Brien; I am Bill's mother. I recently lost my son Ron in Vietnam, that is the reason I am so long in writing. Bill was always a good boy and never gave me trouble. Like all teenagers he wanted to have his own way so since he was fifteen, he went to live with his father. The only time Bill was ever in trouble with the law was when he was thirteen; he was riding his bicycle on the highway, he and Ron and another boy. He appeared in court, before the juvenile judge, they were not fined but were given a good lecture and were very good after that. I appeared with them and they showed very much respect for the judge. As a child Bill was like most other boys. He was a Cub Scout and a Boy Scout and seemed to be well liked by the other children his age. He always got along very well in school. He attended Sunday school and church and took an active part in most activities. Bill was sorry after he left to live with his father and he told me so. He came to see his two younger brothers and sister and always tried to help me with them. I don't know too much about Bill's illness. His father and his wife never let me know anything about my boys when they were sick. I do feel Bill was a wonderful boy and I sure would do all I can for him. I am enclosing a letter Bill wrote to his sister just recently. I would appreciate it if you could return the letter to me, even though he's in trouble himself, he is very considerate of other people . . .

Letters, dozens of letters. I had become involved in the case quite late. The first defense counsel had proceeded on the theory that his client was innocent. O'Brien refused to take a polygraph, and his lawyer became horrified with the thought that he might be representing a guilty man and withdrew. Had I been involved earlier, I would have done many things differently. The case was lost before it was mine, but I did what I could.

In military courts the prosecution first questions each witness to establish his identity. By the time William F. O'Brien took the stand and identified himself, he had heard me read and say good things about him. Since the court had no alternative but to give him a life sentence, and since I already had a deal with the convening authority that only twenty-five years of that would be approved, much of what I was doing was theater for O'Brien's benefit. The court did not know that. They would not find out until right before they adjourned that they would be instructed to return a life sentence. O'Brien was ready, and I called him. He leaned forward in his chair, slumping, pale, the slightest quiver to his hands. As he sat in the witness chair, I remember thinking this must be what people look like when they are strapped into the electric chair.

My questions were simple, short; I hoped my manner was reassuring.

Q: And you're wearing the Combat Medic's badge, aren't you?
A: Yes, sir.

Q: And you earned that over here?
A: Yes, sir, I did.

Q: Why did you extend?
A: Well, sir, they told me that if I extended, my brother wouldn't have to come over here, sir.

Q: You extended with the intent of your brother not coming over here?
A: Yes, sir.

Q: How long did you, had you been in-country, when you went AWOL?
A: About ten and a half months, sir.

Q: Ten and a half months?
A: Yes, sir.

Q: During that time, had you ever taken a leave, before?
A: No, sir.

Q: Had you ever taken an R & R?
A: No, sir.

Q: Did you take an extension leave?
A: No, sir.

Q: Now, why did you go AWOL?

A: Well, a couple of buddies talked me into going to Saigon and staying a few days and I got down there and I got involved with this Vietnam girl and she talked me out of going back, which wasn't right.

Q: You were involved with a Vietnamese girl in Saigon, is that correct?

A: Yes, sir.

Q: When would your DEROS have been?

A: Yesterday.

This was the time for me to pause, shuffle a few papers, sip some water from the plastic cup on my desk, and allow that fact to sink into the jury. DEROS was the date a soldier was to go home, his tour completed. One particularly compassionate medic, who devoted extra time to the medical needs of the local Vietnamese, used to meet with me for a drink, shake his head, and say, "The Vietnamese—they have no DEROS."

Q: Tell us some more about this Vietnamese girl.

A: Well, she always kept a lot of marijuana and dope in her house. She's always wanting a lot of money for her mom, she always wanted money mostly.

Q: Prior to this incident, did you have any convictions of any kind?

A: I had one Article 15, sir.

Q: You had an Article 15, and what was that for?

A: I had an accident at Fort Campbell with a three-quarter ton.

Q: But you had no Article 15s in your 10 months here in-country, is that correct?

A: No, sir.

Q: Do you know how your efficiency reports were?

A: They were excellent, sir.

Q: Now, Bill, I want you to tell the court in your own words about the incident that happened December 2.

A: Well, sir, we went down to this mama-san's house. Well, she was in charge of the black market in the area, we were going to rob her. Well, we went down there, Baker and I went upstairs to transact some business, she thought, and when we got upstairs, we started to hear these screams from downstairs and it seemed like the screams were attracting police and things. When the screams started, the mama-san that I was conducting business with got up and she headed for the stairs. I grabbed her around the neck and stopped her. She couldn't scream. When she finally went limp I lowered her to the floor. Then we heard a shot downstairs. I looked down there and saw that Wilson had shot that other mama-san and Baker, it seemed like, that all those people were all around me. Baker was yelling for me to kill her, stab her, you know. I pulled a knife out of my boot and stabbed her, then we left.

Q: What had you been able to observe of Wilson and the maid downstairs, before you stabbed the mama-san?
A: Well, sir, he was beating on her head with his .45, sir.
Q: You observed Wilson downstairs beating her on the head, is that correct?
A: Yes, sir.

A gruesome story, told without inflection. I wondered if the entire court was getting the same depression headache I had. It struck me that we all wanted to take a nap. None of us wanted to hear any more about this. The court had an obligation to inflict punishment, and they needed to understand the extent to which O'Brien had already been punished.

Q: All right, who picked you up?
A: The Vietnamese police, sir.
Q: Where were you taken?
A: To the Vietnamese jail, sir.
Q: What's it like in a Vietnamese jail?
A: Well, they don't feed you. They feed you one type of vegetable, a small piece of meat and a glass of water every day.
Q: Could you identify the meat?
A: No, sir.
Q: Did you eat it?
A: No, sir.
Q: What were the sanitary conditions like?

A: They were very poor, sir, they had a Vietnamese latrine like
      in a cell, it was all stinkin' and bugs and it was very poor.

This testimony was background but would not elicit sympathy. I moved into the strongest area, the tragic death of his
brother.

Q: Did you request to attend his funeral?
A: Yes, sir.
Q: Were you allowed to do so?
A: No, sir.

I had intentionally kept his testimony very short. There was
no point in entering into any area that would have made him
vulnerable on cross-examination. The prosecuting attorney,
Captain Heaston, was a Nebraska boy, a very vigorous and
effective prosecutor, who sincerely believed that O'Brien should
receive no clemency. I gave my closing argument as if the trial
court had some kind of discretion in the matter. My speech was
long, and I quote a very few excerpts:

A classic, tragic story from Vietnam. A boy who is now nineteen
years has been in this country, I believe he said eighteen months,
would have derosed yesterday. A boy who has otherwise a perfect record and was plunged into an unbelievable nightmare.
The whirlpool of events that swept this young man along in his
involvement with the woman . . .

A combination of drugs and a blind raging moment and now
he's here before you. We do not minimize the nature of this incident. We do not say that it is not tragic. We are not going to
come up with some kind of argument that the woman was a
criminal and needed to be killed anyway. She was a human
being and had a right to live, and she is dead. Without minimiz-
ing the crime, we appeal to the court's mercy. The law officer is
going to instruct you that you have the right and obligation to
return one sentence and one sentence only.

When you come back from findings, you must sentence this
young man to life imprisonment. You have no alternative. You

may not come back and give a lesser sentence. The only sentence
you are allowed to give this young man is life imprisonment. . . .
The law officer will, however, instruct you, that you will have
an additional opportunity to participate in determining some
nature of clemency for this young man and his family. You have
the right to say to the convening authority, we have returned a
sentence, a sentence in this case for life, because the book says
we have to, but we sat here and heard the evidence and now we
want to participate; and therefore we respectfully petition the
convening authority not to approve the sentence that we had
given insofar as it may lead to confinement in excess of twenty
years or fifteen years or ten years or five years or whatever you
think is just and merciful. . . .

I use the term mercy without any apology whatever. Mercy is
not something that a person can earn. Mercy is a gift. It is an
honorable request; there is no disgrace in asking for mercy. . . .
The greatest teacher of all time made this request for all men
and for all time in the book of Saint Matthew, chapter five, verse
seven, when he said, "Blessed are the merciful for they shall
obtain mercy."

My closing argument continued to its conclusion. Quoting
the Bible is risky; it encourages the jury to scrutinize the lawyer
for hints of fraud. I welcomed that scrutiny.

The court returned its verdict as instructed by the judge.
William F. O'Brien was sentenced to life imprisonment. It was
late in the day, and we were all hungry and thirsty. So we all
drifted out in the direction of the officers' club. The night before
we had been under rocket attack, so the club had been closed,
and I hoped that tonight a few of the court members would sit
down with a drink and would listen to me. I did get two peti-
tions that night. One juror petitioned the commanding general
that O'Brien's sentence be reduced to a bad conduct discharge
(rather than dishonorable) and confinement for twelve years.
Another signed a petition for fifteen years. The convening
authority approved a twenty-five year sentence, as I knew he
would. But I had made my record, and people would read that
record.

On November 23, 1971, the Army Court of Military Review

reduced the sentence to fifteen years. On July 2, 1974, O'Brien was released from the United States Disciplinary Barracks on parole. He had spent approximately five years in confinement, the longest time any of my clients has ever been incarcerated. On May 20, 1975, the Army Clemency Board, and the Office of the Secretary of the Army, further reduced his sentence to thirteen years. Similar clemency action reduced his sentence to eleven years on June 23, 1976, and ten years on June 17, 1977. On June 23, 1978, he was released from parole. The time and effort I put into making his appellate record paid off in the end. I am certain those were difficult years for him. I think of his family and his victim's family going through their separate healing processes half a world apart.

Somewhere amid the confusion of justice, and law, and things only peripherally related to either, I had done the best I could, and I took a C-130 back to Saigon, where I caught a helicopter back to the Plantation. In the C-130 there were scout dogs and dog excrement, and a few Vietnamese nationals who were vomiting on the floor. We had all been marched in and told to sit down. Duffle bags were stored at the rear of the plane. A brutal trip by civilian standards, but not out of the ordinary for Vietnam. As I sat on the floor, a tall, thin, black GI from the 101st Airborne Division asked me if I wanted to change places with him. I looked up, puzzled. He explained that some of the duffle bags were about to tumble, that whoever was sitting where I was sitting would have a duffle bag land on him, and that he somehow thought it more appropriate that he be the victim of such an accident than I. He was looking at my collar insignia—not the captain's rank, but the judge advocate branch. "After all, sir, you're a *lawyer*."

IV

Every two weeks, either CWO Wilford Heaton or I would take a helicopter or a truck to Black Horse Base Camp and spend a day and a night there. Word went out that the lawyer was in town, and the men would line up to see us. It was always an enjoyable time for me. Steel helmet, pistol, flak vest, and brief-case complete with Uniform Code of Military Justice, tooth-brush, razor, change of socks and shorts, and lots of yellow pads. Black Horse provided me with courts-martial, as well as other opportunities to provide legal assistance.

The 11th Armed Cavalry Regiment was commanded by Col. George S. Patton III, who was destined to become a general in a few years. He was a striking man, impressive, decisive, and highly intelligent. The base camp was clean, well organized, and generally secure, though there were Viet Cong in the Xuan Loc area. I have no doubt that, as with other combat leaders, he tended to see lawyers as a necessary evil, but he always made us feel welcome. In the morning we would be invited to the com-mand staff meeting, and sometimes captured weapons would be passed around for examination—Viet Cong weapons, many of which I had never previously seen or heard of.

I was generally treated well at the officers' club at Black Horse, where I could get a cold drink and sometimes watch a movie. And, on occasion, I had the opportunity to stay in Colonel Patton's trailer. Why would he yield up his trailer for a traveling lawyer? Because he was out doing what he enjoyed most. Nights he would take an armored vehicle out into harm's way in the hope of drawing fire. The man loved combat, and he was generally revered by his soldiers. Somebody once told me that when Patton was shot, he insisted that his blood-stained jungle fatigue shirt be preserved.

I remember one runner, a Ralph Benson, who was facing discharge, three and one-half years' confinement at hard labor, and total forfeitures. He had asked me to call on his Vietnamese wife sometime when I was in Saigon and to give her what com-fort I could—and to arrange to have her and their child present in court.

I remember her apartment, the faint smell of incense, the curtains drawn against the light and noise, candles in the room, and, somehow in Saigon, a sense of heavy, absolute silence. I felt clumsy, sitting there with my .45 pistol in its holster; my survival knife concealed by my jungle fatigue blouse.

I could sense no real reaction from her, and although she was younger than I, I had the feeling of being a badly schooled youth in the presence of a genuine adult. Or an intruder in a slow motion movie. My God, any minute she was going to offer me cookies and milk, and I was going to say "Yes'm." She did agree to come to the trial. She said there was nothing I could do for her, nothing she required, no message she wanted to send back to her husband, and that she had great confidence in my ability to represent him. I hated to leave. I had sunk into the furniture, and had sunk into the incense and the quietude, and had been drawn into her presence, feeling, as I did, that here was, in some sense, a good home.

I stayed in Saigon that night and got very drunk. I had not known any hotels, so an MP directed me to a hotel, which turned out to be a whorehouse. The girls would sit in an outdoor restaurant in the roof, hustling drinks—Saigon tea. You buy them a cup of tea for two dollars, and they sit with you. On the roof, watching the tracer rounds bleed across the sky above the city until sometime after the eleven o'clock curfew, then down to your room. The girls sat out in the hallway, where they spent the night, if they could not find somebody to share a room. Some of them were attractive, and I was full of gin, but not that drunk.

At his trial, Benson testified:

Q: Pvt. Benson, you've pled guilty to desertion. Why did you
     desert?
A: Because I had a wife and child to support, sir.
Q: Wasn't the army paying you enough?
A: Sir, the army wasn't paying me anything for approximately
     seven months.
Q: Can you explain how this happened?
A: I was detailed from the 11th Armored Cavalry Regiment to
     work with the CI group as an undercover agent. I was sup-

posed to go into a Filipino counterfeit ring and find out
where their ink and paper and prints were that they were
using to print the military payment certificates at this time.
The CI had me put down on my company morning report
as AWOL. In the Saigon area the Filipinos have different
means of finding out just about anything about any individual that would come into their contact. For this reason
they put me down as AWOL on the morning report. I returned to my unit upon one month for pay. I found that the
1st Sgt. had made a mistake and dropped me from the rolls
as a deserter and in turn they had all my finance records
sent to Indianapolis, Indiana.

Q: What did you then do?
A: I returned back to the CI unit in Saigon. This time I stayed
for approximately a month and a half to two months. I
came home from work one evening and my wife had told
me she had to borrow ten P from the houseboy downstairs
to buy a loaf of bread.

At this point, I stopped, turned and looked at his wife, an
Oriental madonna holding their son. She kept her adoring gaze
trained on her husband as she gently stroked her sleeping child.
At such times, a pause of a minute or two in the absolute silence
of the courtroom can seem like hours. I turned back to Benson.

Q: What did you then do?
A: I returned back to my unit and tried to get paid this time,
sir.
Q: And what happened when you returned to your unit to try
to get paid?
A: I went to the officer in charge of the rear detachment and
asked him about getting paid. He said that there was noth-
ing he could do at this time; as far as he was concerned I
was a deserter.
Q: Who did you go to then?
A: I went to the inspector general's office, at the 11th Cavalry.
Q: What did the inspector general tell you?
A: He said that he could give me ten dollars pay and that was
all he could do.
Q: What did you do at this time?

A: I left the next day for Saigon, sir.

Q: You had spoken of your wife and child. Are they present in the courtroom?

A: Yes, sir, that's my wife and child sitting there.

Q: During the time when the army hadn't paid you for seven months or so, did you consider having your wife seek employment?

A: Sir, there's very few decent jobs in Vietnam that women can have.

This was time for another pause, time for me to scribble on a yellow pad, perhaps raise an eyebrow, perhaps look over at the fan. I wanted the members of the court to think about the economic circumstances of that wife and mother in the back of the courtroom. It struck me that I had milked that issue for all it was worth, and it was time for me to move on.

Q: Have you ever been wounded?

A: Yes, sir, three times.

Q: Tell us about the times when you were wounded.

A: First time I was operating a minesweeper, clearing a road for the tank company assigned to the 1st Squadron. We found something in the road and the commander of the tank hollered at me. When I turned I was shot in the back by a sniper.

Q: Did you receive a Purple Heart?

A: Yes, sir, I did.

Q: When was the second time you were wounded?

A: I was reconning an area for an ambush outside the 11th Cav base camp when my driver hit a mine in the APC and I was thrown off.

Q: Did you receive a Purple Heart?

A: Yes, sir.

Q: And what was the third time you were wounded?

A: During the second offensive in Cholon, sir, while working for the Criminal Investigation Department.

Q: And what happened then?

A: I returned home from work one evening. The Viet Cong had taken over the section of Cholon. They had pinned us in the hotel. CI had come down to try to get me out of there for about three days and we were running out of food and water and stuff. I went out to see about getting food and letting people know I was still all right and still down in the Cholon area. I was practically half way around the corner of the hotel when one of the Viet Cong snipers threw a hand grenade out the window and caught me in the ankles with shrapnel.

Q: Did you put in for a Purple Heart for that?
A: Yes, sir, I was. It's still pending at this time.

Q: When you were apprehended, were you confined?
A: Yes, sir, I was.

Q: What was the first place you were locked up?
A: The first place I was confined was at the 716th Military Police Station in Saigon.

Q: And where did you go after that?
A: I was returned to the 1st Squadron that was here at Long Binh. I was confined there in the POW camp, sir.

Q: And who were you with in this POW camp?
A: Two North Vietnamese soldiers.

Q: Were you confined in the same place as two NVA's?
A: Yes, sir, they had a barbed-wire area.

Q: Were you actually in physical contact with them?
A: Yes, sir, I was.

This was the time for the raised eyebrow, the slump of the shoulders, the sad shaking of the head. How could this fine young man have been treated so shabbily by the army? Time to mop the forehead, and to move on to more horror:

Q: Where did you go after that?
A: I went to the USARV Installation Stockade.

Q: Where did you stay when you first got to the USARV Installation Stockade?
A: CONEX container, sir.

Q: Tell us about this CONEX container. Was there any furniture in it?
A: No, sir.

Q: Did you have your own?

A: There was another man in the room with me.

Q: And how about ventilation?

A: They had two strips cut out of the top of the CONEX running the length from top to bottom.

Q: In the course of an ordinary day how much time were you allowed out of that steel box?

A: Approximately forty-five minutes in the morning for PT, for chow, to go out and get chow, come back in and for a ten minute shower in the evening.

Q: Did it ever get warm in there?

A: Yes, sir, extremely.

During the course of the trial, I was able to arrange for Benson and his wife to have some time together. I have a photo of the two of them, and their child, standing in front of the SJA quonset hut, she, striking in her diaphanous *ao dai.*

It occurs to me, in retrospect, that the quiet luxury of her apartment was inconsistent with his testimony of poverty. That is clear to me now thousands of miles and many years away. Benson got a bad conduct discharge (not a dishonorable discharge) and a sentence of a year confinement. He told her he would be back within a year and I am sure he was. I visited him again in the stockade after he was convicted and before he went back to the States, and he told me he had devised a way to get wealthy by smuggling gold through Bangkok to Switzerland. I told him that I wished him good luck in life and bad luck in his criminal endeavors.

I am certain that he did return to Saigon, probably by the very beginning of 1970. I wish him well and wonder what became of him, and his wife and his child.

In representing runners, brevity was the soul of discretion. Court members were frantic to get back to the units for their "real work." It served my clients to keep their testimony brief; there was a very real danger in opening doors to cross-examination. Since normally cross-examination will be confined to the scope of direct examination, proper witness preparation had to do with making certain that the witness told the truth, but did not stray into dangerous areas. This was crucial during the trial of David R. Johanssen, who was charged with AWOL and currency violations.

David lived on Tru Minh Ky, with his Vietnamese "wife." She was a compulsive gambler, and his dependency on her was as intense as her addiction to gambling: his life had become a scramble to keep her happy. He supported her by doing odd jobs for criminal gangs in Saigon, including a Philippine gang, a gang from India, and an organization from Cholon, Saigon's Chinatown.

He told me: "Well, I walk behind this screen and I don't see this guy's face but he give me five thousand pee (piasters) and a picture and an address and I go kill the dude and then go get my other five thousand." Johanssen was big, muscular, almost formidable but for the twinkle in his eyes, sly half-grin, engaging shrug of the shoulders. He never said "aw shucks," but I was afraid he was going to try. He was born in rural Illinois and orphaned before his first birthday. He was adopted by foster parents, who then divorced when he was five, and he bounced from home to home until he completed the eighth grade, when he joined the Job Corps. Although he scored very low on his GT, he was no dummy. A swashbuckler, a deserting soldier of fortune.

His numerous charges carried a possible sentence of dishonorable discharge and confinement for fifty-nine years. The thought of being sent back to America in confinement seemed to delight him in an eerie sort of way; he once showed me a picture of Kim, his wife on Tru Minh Ky, and she was at least twice his age, and when he spoke of her, his words were tainted by disgust. Johanssen would always be a hostage of somebody or something—operating in daredevil fashion within whatever prison he found for himself. I never met Kim, but I saw her picture and I heard him speak of her, and I am certain that she is, this very moment, putting some poor devil through unshirted hell.

Benson had originally been arrested for having stolen money from a civilian in a bar. After the office of the provost marshal had arrested him, an alert clerk discovered that the CI wanted Johanssen for currency violations, a crime that was inevitable, arising as it did from the remorseless dynamics of Gresham's law. In order to preserve the Vietnamese currency, our government had made an artificial legal rate of exchange: one hundred and ten piasters for an American dollar, whether in green or military pay certificates. The green dollar could always get at least four or five hundred piasters on the black market exchange; the military pay certificate could always get at least two hundred or two hundred fifty pee; the law-abiding GI was, as they say, getting shortchanged. So if a GI sold one dollar in military pay certificates for a few hundred piasters, he could take those piasters back to the base and exchange them for two dollars in military pay certificates, which could then be sold for over four hundred piasters, and it was merely a matter of moving your money from place to place and doubling its value every time.

But then, what to do with all the military pay certificates? You could purchase a money order, which would be honored by banks everywhere, and the money order could be cashed in for dollars at various banks throughout the world. So a military directive was passed: no GI could purchase over two hundred dollars per month in money orders. In order to purchase a money order you had to fill out a form stating that. Falsely filling out the form was a separate offense.

At the time of his arrest for theft in the bar, Johanssen had been going to and from military installations with his piasters, military pay certificates, and money orders, using money that belonged to a notorious Vietnamese known as Mr. Lo. Johanssen had been keeping 10 percent of the money he got for Mr. Lo as his payment. According to the records of the CI, Johanssen had purchased money orders in the sum of just over fifteen hundred dollars on behalf of Mr. Lo. Johanssen's earnings were one hundred fifty dollars.

By the time I got to see Johanssen, he had made a valid and

admissible confession (fleeing the Dragon Lady?) and had voluntarily given up handwriting exemplars which had been for-
warded to Japan, where the document examiners had verified
that it had, in fact, been Johanssen who signed those money
orders and their affiliated documents.

I wanted to get Johanssen in and out of court as quickly as
possible, though I wanted to make certain the court was aware
of his limited intellect and education, as well as his sordid child-
hood.

Q: Specialist Johanssen, how old are you?
A: Nineteen.

Q: What is your GT score?
A: Eighty-four, sir.

Q: How many years of education did you have?
A: Eight years, sir.

Q: Did you complete eighth grade?
A: Yes, sir.

Q: Are your parents living?
A: No, sir.

Q: At what age did you become an orphan?
A: Before I was one year old.

Q: Were you then adopted?
A: Yes, sir.

Q: And did you live with your foster parents?
A: Yes, sir.

Q: For how long did you live with them?
A: 'Til I was about five.

Q: What happened then?
A: They got a divorce.

Q: And which one did you live with?
A: I stayed with my mother.

Q: For how long?
A: 'Til I was about seven.

Q: And what happened then?
A: Then I went out to a farm with my father.

Q: And how long did you stay with him?
A: I stayed with him until I was about eleven or twelve.

Q: And then what happened?
A: I went back in town with my mother.
Q: How long did you stay with your mother?
A: 'Til I was about thirteen.
Q: And what happened then?
A: I went back to the farm with my father 'til I was about fifteen.
Q: Why did you leave then?
A: Well, I left because my father's wife was beating me one day with a broom handle, and I ran away.
Q: And where did you go?
A: I went back in town with my mother.
Q: How long did you stay with your mother?
A: I stayed with her 'til just before I went in the Job Corps.
Q: How old was that?
A: Sixteen.
Q: And why did you leave?
A: Well, my mother was drinking heavily one night and this man molested her and as a result of that I went to help her, and the man ended up in the hospital.

I remember when the court retired to deliberate. Sitting at counsel table with your client is a time for reassurance, a certain amount of hand-holding. There are frequent trips to the water cooler, and courtroom proceedings can speed up the bowels more than a rocket attack (but less than a malaria pill), and my driver always had to accompany my waiting client to an outhouse.

But Johanssen did not need to drink, nor did he need to go to the outhouse, nor did he need to have his hand held. He was enjoying himself. The trial was, for him, a kind of a social event. And when he and I arose and approached the court together, standing at attention and saluting the president of the court, Johanssen seemed delighted that the court announced a sentence of a bad conduct discharge and four years' confinement.

He was grinning as they led him out of the courtroom, and I was still trying to gather my composure when the law officer said, "Does the government have any other cases to bring before this court at this time?" and the prosecution said, "Yes, sir. I recommend a fifteen minute recess so that we can prepare for the next trial," and the law officer then asked me if I was counsel for the next accused and if fifteen minutes was enough time to get ready, and I answered "Yes, sir" to both questions. Ah, youth!

Of course there were many kinds of AWOL. The man who simply disappeared from his unit for a short visit to a local town was seldom brought to trial unless he was a chronic troublemaker. It is, after all, a characteristic of the military that an unauthorized leaving of a job is a crime. Life on the Plantation, where I was stationed, was generally uneventful. I knew many people who would try to walk through the PX on their lunch hour so they could see the luxuries and appliances that reminded them of the World, or perhaps so they could see the Vietnamese women who operated the checkout counters. Any break in routine became somewhat of a dream and even an obsession with some of the men. A few enterprising GIs had taken one of the rear bunkers (The House of the Rising Sun) and had engaged a few day workers to sell "short time." There had been no pimping involved; none of the men was making any money from it. They just wanted a chance to have women available to themselves and to their friends. The discovery of this "vice ring" had led to some minor nonjudicial punishment.

"Airborne runs" in the villages surrounding Bien Hoa were fairly common. A soldier would check out a jeep and drive through town at a very slow rate, and when he passed a whorehouse, the passengers would leap from the back of the jeep, run in, and be standing in the street ready to jump back in when the jeep returned. And there were Vietnamese women who worked evenings in the officers' club. Some of the men would climb into the back of the truck that took the girls home and tumble out of the back of the truck near where the girls got out. Of course, that could not be done unless one also had made arrangements to sneak back on post in some other vehicle the next morning. Such offenses were seldom prosecuted, unless they led to missing duty, or unless the perpetrators were known troublemakers whom the command would have liked to have prosecuted anyway.

I knew one young officer who had fallen (he said) deeply in love with one of the waitresses at our officers' club. She had told him that he could come to her house if he would bring an expensive fan from the PX and leave it at her house. She had, in her broken English, given him incomplete instructions as to how to get to her house. He later related a night of running around from house to house, in an area in which there were at least some VC, knocking on doors at midnight, holding a fan hopefully in his hand, until he finally found her place. If such cases had been prosecuted, there would have been no time for any other phase of military justice.

So the system worked as follows: a commander would receive a report of an infraction, anywhere from failure to salute to a serious crime. He could (in minor offenses) choose simply to lecture the offender. Or, he could offer "nonjudicial punishment" under Article 15 of the Uniform Code of Military Justice. If the accused chose to accept punishment under Article 15, he might be fined, given extra duty, or even lose a stripe.

The next step up from Article 15 was a summary court-martial (usually invoked after nonjudicial punishment had been offered and refused), a hearing of limited powers. Then the special court-martial, in which lawyers were used. Special courts could give up to six months' confinement and a bad conduct discharge and were taken seriously. Most of my time was spent defending in general courts-martial or appearing in the Article 32 (preliminary) hearings that made up the basis for the staff judge advocate's pretrial advice to the (command) convening authority, who finally issued the orders for trial.

One of my runners was Hal Joseph, a tall muscular blonde with a kind of cool laziness. He was a Californian and eager to mention that fact. In every war movie I have ever seen, there is a Hal Joseph swaggering along the trail, carrying a heavy

weapon over a shoulder, swinging the free arm, cool in the face
of certain peril.

My main problem had been to convince Joseph he was not
going to win the court over by cooling them out, and that
although his muscular slouch was without a doubt de rigueur in
Southern California, a little starch and snap would sell better
with the court. Away we went:

Q: Did you initially volunteer to come here?
A: Yes, sir, I did.

Q: And did you extend voluntarily?
A: Yes, sir, I did.

Q: And I see you're wearing the CIB. Did you get that here?
A: Yes, sir, I did.

Q: What has been your job here in Vietnam?
A: I came into Vietnam, sir, with my unit. I'm a scout tracker,
    machine gun; then from there I went into the mortar section
    and I was the chief computer, section leader for about three
    to six 9-gun batteries. The chief computer was responsible
    for where the rounds fell and any ambush patrols or people
    in the area at the time I was firing.

Q: Give us some the places you were in combat.
A: Junction City One, the Iron Triangle, Hobo Woods—a few
    other operations.

Q: You were absent without proper authority from 11 August
    until 9 October this year, were you not?
A: Yes, sir.

Q: How did it happen that you went absent without leave?
A: Well, sir, I came in off the line—I was due to rotate, and my
    replacement came. At this time I was informed that I was
    going to the headquarters unit mess hall to be permanent
    KP for the thirty-five days before I rotated.

Q: I see. You were told that you would be a permanent KP
    until your DEROS in thirty-five days, is that correct?
A: Yes, sir.

Q: What did you do?
A: I took some of my clothing from the club; I moved down to
    the security guard barracks.

Q: How many days have you been in the stockade as of today?
A: Eighty-one, sir.

I had avoided any area in which there could be potential embarrassment. The prosecution did not have properly certified or authenticated records of the two prior convictions for AWOL, and it was important that I give him no opportunity to get them into evidence through cross-examination. I could get whatever I needed through other witnesses. There was, for instance, a Sergeant Ellingsworth, who testified that he had known Specialist Joseph as a squad leader in a mortar squad, that he served with him in combat for about six months, that Joseph was a brave and good soldier, handled responsibilities well, and that Ellingsworth would give Joseph a mortar squad again if he could have him back.

If the people who served with a man were willing to have him back with them in combat, it told the court more about the soldier than anything else I could have brought up. Joseph could have received a dishonorable discharge and two years' incarceration but this court gave him a suspended sentence of six months, so his only real punishment was his time in pretrial confinement, plus a forfeiture of ninety-seven dollars per month for six months. He was allowed to stay in the army.

Joseph had never much wanted to discuss his offense, presumably on the grounds that it was not cool to do so, but during our time in the stockade, he liked to read me his poems. He wrote short poems in a kind of jumpy iambic tetrameter, irregular rhyme schemes, about the fact that he was fighting for freedom, etc. Some of his poems were published in a regular column in *Stars and Stripes*, called "Boondocks Bards." I had been able to "borrow" a few volumes of poetry from a post library somewhere or other and smuggle them into the stockade for Joseph's birthday, December 25. He was delighted.

Joseph asked me to send his poems to some small magazines in the States and I did, and some of them were published. But more often than not I would receive an enraged note from the editor, bitter that Joseph's poems deviated from the orthodoxy. He wrote of heroism; the editors demanded atrocities. He was fairly cheerful at a time when the editors required catatonia. He insisted on writing of his reality rather than of the editors' nightmares.

He had an informal collection of his verse called *The Whistling Leper.* I have never been in a leper colony, and I do not know if there are such things as whistling lepers, but I do know that if Joseph were a leper, he would be a whistling leper. He was a man who knew the facts of life and who refused to whimper—an anachronism certainly and, in the late sixties, a social leper. He shook my hand and left for his unit to process out and head back to the World. I told him Bob Jones was giving me New Year's Eve in Saigon. He said, "I dare you to write a poem about it." So I did.

NEW YEAR'S EVE, 1968

Beyond Blackhorse, Xuan Loc
and Rock Village,
in a smaller town north

We had a hearing on a shooting;
the villagers
loved dai uy mop

Applauded my every gesture,
and booed the interpreter,
drinking coke

in my makeshift courtroom.
One client
(found not guilty)

gave me his pin:
Wine, women, bodycount.
At firebase Tiger

My head was split and sewed.
My hooch maid scraped the blood
Off my pillow, said

"V.C. numba ten."
Drunk in Saigon
I march to my hotel

Singing "Georgy Girl"
late in a dark street
weeks before Tet.

V

I was occasionally ordered to prosecute, and that was always difficult for me. I do not mean to denigrate the prosecutorial function; God knows, we could not have a working adversary system without good prosecutors. I have spent enough time justifying the role of defense counsel in our system of justice, that I would be hard pressed to attack either the role of prosecutor, or the prosecutors themselves. I have known many prosecutors who were gentle, wise, compassionate, and guided by a desire to help people.

But the act of prosecution seems mildly foreign to my nature. Without prosecutors, there could be no defense counsel; there could be no criminal trials. There would be chaos, and civilized society would be destroyed. Prosecution was difficult for me, but I did prosecute when I was ordered to and did my best, no matter how inept I may have seemed.

There was, however, one kind of case that was harder for me than prosecution. It was defending an American soldier who had turned his rifle or his knife on a fellow American. Killing a fellow soldier, one whose duty it is to trust and rely on you, is, to me at least, a form of fratricide. I will be accused of flag waving; I plead guilty without remorse.

And there is a deeper and more personal reason why this kind of case is abhorrent to me. A relative of mine—a very fine, handsome, athletic young man, and the son of a favorite cousin —was murdered by a fellow GI in Vietnam, some months before I arrived. I quote from an official document:

On 4 March 1968, at about 2030 hours, Specialist 5 Robert L. Jones, RA Headquarters and Headquarters Company 2/2 Infantry, 1st Infantry Division allegedly shot Specialist 5 John W. Stevens, Jr., in the chest with a .45 caliber pistol. Investigation reveals that SP5 Jones, while in the 173d NCO Club, became involved in an argument with Sergeant Kenneth Bradley, HHC, 2/2 Inf 1st Inf Div, and decided to go outside the club to fight. SGT Bradley and SP5 Jones removed their pistols, placed them on the floor and went outside the club. After getting outside the club, SGT Bradley and SP5 Jones decided to talk over the argument and at this time, several personnel assigned to the 173d Assault Helicopter Company also went outside the club to see if a fight were started, no damage would be done to the club. A fight started between members of the 173d and 2/2 Infantry. SP5 Jones left the immediate area, walked into the club, picked up his weapon and stated he was leaving. SP5 Jones left the club, walked up to where SP5 Stevens was standing and allegedly made the statement, "I know how to break up this fight" at which time he put his hand on SP5 Sevens's chest, raised his pistol and fired one round at the chest of SP5 Stevens. The bullet fired by SP5 Jones first struck Jones's left hand, then entered the chest of SP5 Stevens who fell to the ground. SP5 Jones stepped back after firing the shot and stated "Who's next, how about you in the white tee shirt?" After the shot was fired, the fight broke up and SP5 Jones left and again entered the NCO Club and stated. "I shot the wrong man." Then, SP5 Jones gave his pistol to the Club Custodian after removing the magazine. SP5 Stevens was immediately transported by ambulance to CO B, 1st Medical Rogers. SP5 Jones was air evacuated to the 93d Evacuation Hospital at Long Binh, RVN for treatment and surgery. He was further evacuated to Japan for medical treatment.

Specialist Jones, who murdered John Stevens, happened to be black. By the very nature of things, many of my clients in similar cases would be black. Should I pretend that the lingering horror and grief of John Stevens's murder was not an indelible part of my emotional makeup? The shock of John's murder did inform my perceptions of law and of Vietnam. But my reaction did not, I believe, diminish my professional efforts: the broken heart would not waste the quotidian skills. Specialist Jones had been prosecuted, convicted, given a dishonorable discharge, and sentenced to confinement at hard labor—I am certain that he received excellent assistance of defense counsel, to which he was entitled.

Jimmie Roosevelt had requested me as his defense counsel. He was charged with assault to commit murder on one man, assault with a dangerous weapon on a second party, and assault with a dangerous weapon on a third party.
He was black.
His victims were white.
Jimmie was twenty-six years old and had grown up in rural Alabama. He had six sisters and three brothers, and after his mother died, he quit high school to help support the family. He was from an artillery battalion located on Duster Compound, contiguous to the Plantation. He had a previous conviction by summary court-martial for the offense of robbery, and the maximum sentence he could receive for his new offense would be thirteen years' confinement.
Jimmie Roosevelt wrote a poem:

> Sunday March 9, 1969
>
> This is Just The Way i Feel
>
> I am a long ways from Home
> i lay in my Jail cell both
> day and night. My heart
> is fill with pain and my
> soul is fill with sorrow.
> My eyes is dim from
> weeping. They tell me a man not suppose to cry
> but these tears are mine
> is tears are sorrow.
> Every night i flood my
> bunk with my weeping
> and can get no rest
> by day. i am in a world
> are trouble. So i just
> lay here in this old
> cell block waiting to

be trial. if I had
my freedom i would cry
tears of joy. i have
and just about to lose
my mind . . .

There is a tavern in Latham, Nebraska; excellent prime rib
for seven dollars; rural mid-America atmosphere. A very good
bar it is, with its aggressively friendly owner. Gilbert Maschmeier was not always the owner and proprietor of the Latham
Tavern on the Nebraska-Kansas border. I knew him as Sgt. Gilbert Maschmeier, who served under me, and who, as an armed
guard, escorted his prisoner—my client—to Tokyo with me for
depositions. Maschmeier had been previously stationed in
Japan, and—doubly fortunate!—our depositions were set for
the middle of March 1969.

St. Patrick's Day in Tokyo! Trust Sergeant Maschmeier to
discreetly cover the irons that secured Roosevelt to him—using
a field jacket to disguise Jimmie Roosevelt's state of incarceration, during the commercial flights from Vietnam to Tokyo and
back to Vietnam. Trust Sergeant Maschmeier to find us a Yoko-
hama bar called Duffy's Tavern, with a stunning Japanese
woman at the piano, playing "When Irish Eyes Are Smiling!"

Trust Sergeant Maschmeier to become a character witness
for the defense during the court-martial itself!

The case was lengthy, but the theories of the parties were
simple. The prosecution submitted that on February 13, 1969,
shortly before midnight, Jimmie Roosevelt was engaged in a fist-
fight with a soldier named Roman. A noncommissioned officer
broke up the fight, and Roosevelt said, "I'll kill him. I'll kill
him. He won't live through the night."

According to the prosecution, about ten minutes later
Jimmie Roosevelt appeared in the doorway of the orderly room
of the machine gun battery. This time Roosevelt was bleeding
from the right eye and said, "Who hit me?" The sergeant who
had earlier broken up the fight told Roosevelt to take it easy,
and Roosevelt then opened fire with a rifle. The first round hit

Specialist Roman, and the second round struck Sergeant Eaton on the lower back.

Jimmie told me that on the night in question he had been attacked for no reason. He was severely beaten and suffered a swollen eye and cuts to the head and back. (When I first became involved in the case, Roosevelt was very badly bruised, and I immediately had him photographed, and those pictures were offered into evidence.)

Jimmie testified that some people broke up the fight, but that Roman, who was beating Roosevelt at the time, then knocked cold one of the people who broke up the fight. After the fight was broken up, Jimmie went to his quarters, picked up his rifle, went outside, and washed his face. He had carried a loaded rifle to prevent himself from being beaten again. He opened the door to the orderly room and asked for the person who beat him up. At that time he saw Roman coming to his right and he shot him. He fired a few more rounds when the commotion after the first round made him think that other people were attacking him. According to his testimony, Roosevelt never intended to kill or injure anybody. After the shooting, he went to the battalion headquarters and surrendered his rifle to an officer. The case was prosecuted by Maj. Jon Kulish, an excellent and respected lawyer.

At the outset of the trial, the law officer became concerned about the fact that the case was prosecuted by a major and defended by a captain. It is, or at least was in those days, a fairly common practice for the prosecution to outrank the defense counsel, but the military judge wanted to make certain that the record reflected that being represented by a captain was not prejudicial to the defense.

The judge addressed me: "Well, I know you by reputation. I've seen you in action, but I want to make certain that the record indicates one side is not overshadowed by the other."

The question of rank in military justice has given rise to a certain amount of hysteria over the years. People who have criticized military justice have usually done so in a vacuum. Lawyers experienced in trying criminal cases before both civilian and military courts would generally prefer to defend cases before a military court. This is not merely my view; it has been written by many distinguished trial attorneys. There are many reasons for this, and I surmise that one of them has, in fact, to do with the matter of rank. Military judges tend to bear their authority extremely well.

If a man is a colonel, he is accustomed to being saluted and to being treated with courtesy. He does not have the shock of being removed from practice and suddenly placed behind the bench. The military judge has had years of being saluted and of returning the salute; he is both a soldier and a judge, and he knows that discourtesy and unfair behavior are the mark of a weak officer. The military judge has had the advantage of having been promoted through a fairly structured system; he is supremely unlikely to contract Black Robe Fever.

Black Robe Fever is, of course, that dread disease which may destroy the integrity of any judge—state or federal. A judge who prides himself on being inconsiderate and discourteous to the point of being tyrannical has contracted the Fever, and it is fatal: it leads to the death of the mind. The Fever is fairly rare in all places, but it is more common among civilian judges than it is among military judges.

The Roosevelt case moved on apace. During my extensive cross-examination of the surgeon, he admitted he could not tell whether the bullet wounds were direct or the result of a ricochet. This was important to my theory of intent, but the surgeon hurt us: testimony of blood loss secondary to high-velocity missile wound, testimony of surgical removal of approximately 85 percent of a stomach, testimony of removal of the left kidney, and of damage to other organs.

This case on the merits went on through witness after witness. Finally, Jimmie was found not guilty of intent to commit murder, but guilty of intent to commit voluntary manslaughter, on the first charge. He was found guilty of one of the two counts of assault and not guilty on the other one. We went into the sentencing portion, and once again I put him on the stand and did the best I could. During the sentencing hearing his previous offense came to light:

Q: Jimmie, now it's been brought into evidence that you had a previous conviction in a summary court which came to a sixty-day restriction and a written admonition says you took some money from some boys. Now why'd you take that money?

A: Well, sir, I was shooting a few dice with a few of the fellows and some of them were from other units and as I left out of the room I noticed that they changed dices so I got five more dollars and got back in the crap games and I saw them change dices on me again so I told them to let me see the dice. "No," I said, "let me see the dice or give me my money back." So they threw the money down, jumped up and told the man I was trying to rob them.

Q: Have you had occasion to think about these offenses that happened on 13 February?

A: Yes, sir. Think about it every day.

Q: What have been your thoughts on the subject?

A: My thoughts have been sorry, sir. Sergeant Eaton was one of my good friends, me and him pulled guard together. Many a night we sat up 'til two or three o'clock on guard talking. Every time I think about it, it really hurts me. Also with Specialist Roman, you know when I saw him in the hospital in Japan I went over there and shook his hand and I said I hope he gets well soon.

I then called sixteen character witnesses on Jimmie's behalf, the final one being Sergeant Maschmeier.

Jon Kulish was an excellent prosecutor. The court was impressed with him, and I knew Jimmie would be facing confinement. His case followed the normal review process, and he ended up with a dishonorable discharge and thirty months' confinement. He said he was satisfied with my representation. I had done the best I could.

But what of John Stevens? It was natural that he would have been on a helicopter crew. He was born in 1945, while his father was still in the Army Air Corps. His grandfather, Wade

Stevens, had been a pilot in France during World War I and had later been one of America's first commercial pilots before devoting full time to being a lawyer.

I was seven years older than John Stevens, and as he was the son of a favorite cousin, it was natural that I would pay close attention to him as he grew up. His senior year in high school, he played fullback at Washington High School in Phoenix and set two new school records: most yards gained in one season and most yards gained in one game. That same year, he was the Arizona state wrestling champion in the 180-pound division and competed on the state championship track team.

After high school he made his way up to Alaska, where he became an assistant hunting guide. He was a vigorous, hand-some youth, and I cherished his company. His father advised him that if a man was needed by his country, he should go forth and do his duty. So John went into the army with that attitude, was a good soldier, received a dozen Air Medals and a Bronze Star for rescuing comrades under fire, and had an enjoyable R & R in Australia, where he went hunting in the Outback.

I remember his sense of humor; his quiet but serious integrity; his vigorous presence. These years later, I miss him. At least he was spared ever being caught up in a cocktail party discussion about Vietnam.

I was always surprised and flattered to receive letters from my clients.

The letters usually devoted a line or two to thanking me or complimenting me on my performance. That task disposed of, letters invariably went on to ask a favor: a job reference, a letter of explanation, something.

But Murphy's letter was different. As with many of the others, it came from the federal penitentiary at Fort Leaven-worth, Kansas. The letter was lighter and more literate than the others: "We have just finished our midmorning brunch of eggs Benedict and Bloody Marys—time for a short meeting of the J. S. Berry Fan Club, before we have to choose between the ballet and the symphony. Sam (the knife) Gomez has sent his warmest salutations to you—and the rest of the club will drink a toast in your honor at Happy Hour . . ."

The letter was several pages, handwritten with a kind of a flourish, and it was easy to imagine Murphy writing it—hair as black and skin as light as O'Brien, his glasses slipping down his nose, his nervous habit of pushing the glasses back up on the ridge of his nose, tendency to blink before speaking, and to punctuate each sentence with a quick smile.

The letter went on: "Seriously, I had not realized how good a job you had done for me until I saw the lengthy sentences most of the men here received for real chickenshit offenses—I had not realized how competent you were, but perhaps you had underestimated me also; perhaps you had not known that I am a genuinely altruistic person, and that you and I are kindred spirits. . . ."

Kindred spirits. I wonder. The letter closed with the one request I could not fulfill—that I be his friend, and send him a social letter from time to time. I had enjoyed his letter, but in those days even a small act of friendship seemed an enormous burden. I would very much like to see Specialist Murphy again.

December 2, 1968. Murphy had been drinking. He was tired, angry and confused. He stumbled across Blackhorse Base Camp to the headquarters of the 541st Military Intelligence Detachment. He saw two of his best friends sitting, playing cards. He drew his .45 and ordered one of the men, a Staff Sergeant Alawain, to stand up. Alawain tried to comply and Murphy slammed the pistol across Alawain's forehead. Sergeant St. Arnold jumped up, and Murphy fired.

When we went to trial, Murphy was charged with both assaults and faced a six-year sentence. He was my most articulate client, and I knew he would be a good witness. Before I called him, I had taken the testimony of two officers, who had told the court that Murphy was an excellent soldier, proficient in many areas of military intelligence, and a particularly good interrogator. When Murphy testified, his answers tended to be a little on the long side, but the court followed him, fascinated by his sheer intensity:

Q: And what have your duties been since you arrived in Vietnam?

A: I was assigned to the 3d Squadron of the 11th Armored Cavalry Regiment where I eventually became the chief enlisted interrogator and my duties were simply gaining as much information about the enemy from prisoners of war or any other sources, and process it into ordinary intelligence.

Q: Can you give us some examples from your work which give the court a little better idea of what you were doing? Anything in particular about your work you would like to tell us in the field?

A: I've interrogated over two hundred prisoners since I've been in Vietnam and I've screened countless detainees. Many of them were guerrillas and local area guerrillas; they didn't provide large amounts of intelligence but on one occasion I was able to establish a number of facts. And on another occasion he led us to a large weapons cache, recoilless rifles, two mortars, small weapons cache. On another occasion I worked with the Chieu Hoi. This was in the area of Blackhorse Base Camp. He took us out and led us to a base camp and we found mines, large quantities of medicine. These were things that resulted in tangible things, I mean, that we captured. On many other occasions we got information, order-of-battle information. On one occasion, which I was proud of, a prisoner helped us locate the Du Nang regiment. This was during my last tour with the 3d Squadron. . . .

Q: Now I want you to tell us to the best of your knowledge what happened on the evening of December 2 and the morning of December 3 of last year.

A: I spent a very ordinary day. I had just come back from the field. I'd been to finance, was getting my gear squared away. I went to dinner or supper with several other enlisted men from my detachment at the mess hall at the Blackhorse Base Camp. I didn't return to the detachment area with the men I had come with. I went to the 11th Armored Cavalry Noncommissioned Officers' Club. . . . During the time I was

there I received a phone call from Lieutenant Zirities. . . .
He was departing for the U.S. the next day. He invited me to
come to an affair, a farewell party that was being held for
him at the 3d Squadron Officers' Club. So I left the club
and went over to the MI detachment area where I lived and
changed clothing, put on a clean shirt.

Q: Now let me interject a question. During the half hour or
forty-five minutes that you were in the noncommissioned
officers' club, how much scotch did you have to drink?

A: I drank approximately six double scotches.

Q: Six double scotches in a period of a half hour to forty-five
minutes?

A: That's correct, sir. . . .

Q: And did you have anything at the party to drink?

A: Yes, I did.

Q: And what was that?

A: I drank a drink which is more or less a tradition of the 3d
Squadron called an RPG. It's like a Bloody Mary except it
has an added ingredient in addition to vodka and tomato
juice. It has beer in it.

Q: And how long did you remain at this party?

A: 'Til approximately midnight or shortly after midnight. . . .

Q: What then happened?

A: Well, I remember leaving the club because I was despon-
dent. I knew Lieutenant Zirities very well and I was extremely fond of him. I was happy that he was going back to
the States; I was sorry he was leaving.

Q: Take your time. [What do you do with a crying witness?
The only solution I have ever come up with was to tell them
to take their time.]

A: I returned to the aviation section and picked up my hat and
my weapon and I drove back to the detachment area where
I live. And I went to the charge-of-quarters office in the
orderly room and he was asleep.

I was going to talk to him and he was asleep; so I went
down to the company detachment street, and I saw the
lights on in the noncommissioned officers' area. I heard
voices there. I went in. I don't know why I went in; I didn't
have any intention of going in, but I went in and then I . . .
there was a lot of confusion and a lot of trouble and there

> was a struggle and Special Agent Morton yelled at me, "Bill
> St. Arnold's been shot!" I remember my weapon discharge,
> struggling for the weapon. Everybody left, out of the build-
> ing. Major Foley, the CO, called me; I called him; we
> talked; I put the weapon down. I went outside. . . .
>
> Q: Since this incident have you have an occasion to seek any
> psychiatric help?
> A: I've seen the psychiatrist in the USARV Installation Stock-
> ade.
> Q: And did he indicate to you that some psychiatric treatment
> might be of benefit to you?
> A: He said I had deep personal problems and a dependent per-
> sonality, and that I was fortunate that I was intelligent
> enough to profit from psychoanalysis, and I'd have to
> select it on my own, and alcohol complicated it. I would
> profit from it.

The court sentenced Murphy to a year, but they did not give him a dishonorable discharge. He may have gone ahead and made the service a career. I do not know. Nor do I know, in retrospect, how he reacted to my failure to answer his letter. He had asked for my friendship and I had not responded. I hope he found something to do with his wit and intelligence— I trust Sergeant St. Arnold has fully recovered from his bullet wound.

Col. George S. Patton III was an excellent officer and a generous host; I was not certain I wanted him acting as president of the Gomez court-martial.

From the voir dire:

> CAPTAIN BERRY: Colonel Patton, sir. If the law officer advises
> you that the rule of law is: that if a man is in reasonable fear of
> his life or grievous bodily harm he may use any force he con-
> siders necessary to protect himself, could you follow this in-
> struction?
> COLONEL PATTON: Run that by me again.

JUDGE: Just let me emphasize one more thing, too. As I mentioned previously the law officer will give you the law of the case and that's the only law that you may consider.

COLONEL PATTON: Now as I understand it, you rule on that question, right?

JUDGE: I will fully instruct the court. Now the question the defense counsel is asking you is whether you'll be able to follow my instruction. Do you want to ask the question again?

CAPTAIN BERRY: Yes, sir. Colonel Patton, sir. If the law officer advised you that the law is this: a man who is in reasonable fear of his life or grievous bodily harm may use any force he considers necessary to protect himself, could you follow this instruction?

COLONEL PATTON: Yes. Having faith in the law officer, I can follow that instruction upon his advice.

I had no doubt that Colonel Patton would keep his word and would follow the instructions. One great advantage of the court-martial is that its members generally do understand their duties, and they labor mightily to fulfill them.

I have long promulgated this heresy: the members of a military court are likely to be more intelligent, more diligent, and more compassionate than the members of a civilian jury. Samuel Gomez was going to need all the compassion he could get — and then some. He was charged with assaulting a sergeant with intent to commit murder, and assaulting Specialist George Urquhart with a knife. There was no doubt that my client shot his own sergeant in the back; and no doubt that he pulled a knife on Urquhart. There was a sticky racial element to the case: the witnesses against Gomez were black; Gomez and his chief witness were Hispanic. But what to do about Colonel Patton?

He and I had got off to a bad start that morning. The stockade had neglected to have Gomez ready when our jeep and guard had gone to pick him up. The members of the court were angry over the delay. They had come, all of them, by helicopter; they had left their duties in order to sit as jurors. The resentment was obvious. They wanted to be back with their men, fighting a

war. The delay in beginning the trial made them restless. Patton
called me over. "Captain—what the hell's the hang-up?"

Well, I couldn't answer. I could not answer that the trial
had been delayed because of a mistake at the stockade; to do so
would have been to admit that the defendant was, in fact, in
pretrial confinement. The court had no right to know that.
Everybody on the court knew that when a man is charged with
a crime, his command generally has the right to keep him at
work or to give him some kind of pretrial restriction or to have
him confined. The decision to have a man confined was an expression of command judgment. There was no way I would let
the members of the court know that somebody familiar with the
facts of the case and in command of my client had made that
decision.

But Patton was on to me. He whipped out his pistol and
extended it, handle first, toward me. "Here, Captain, take this
and go over the stockade and bring him over here yourself. Let's
get on with the trial." I decided I wanted no more to do with the
members of the court until the trial began, so I grabbed my cap
and went stomping out of the courtroom. Unfortunately, the
chief of staff happened to be passing by, and he complimented
me on my promotion. Curious (but already apprehensive), I
removed my hat. No captain's bars, but the eagle of the full
colonel: I had walked off with Patton's hat! Before the trial
began, I had requested that Patton remove his firearm. The law
officer backed me up on that one.

"The accused respectfully and peremptorily challenges
Colonel Patton." The reason I used my one peremptory chal-
lenge to get Patton off the court was that he was too dominant a
personality. Defense counsel must at least try to dominate the
courtroom. I have no doubt that Colonel Patton would have
been an excellent juror and an excellent president of the court.
But it was obvious that the case would be easier to try without
him.

It was a hot night at the Fishnet Factory. The full moon

made the bunker appear even more stark than usual. Gomez was still dizzy from the afternoon beer, still angry from the fight he had been in, still afraid. He heard a sound from where Sergeant Buchanan was, and he turned and fired.

The Fishnet Factory was the 199th Light Brigade forward command post. The rear command post was Camp Red Ball, which was adjacent to the Plantation. The Redcatchers had only one legal officer assigned: Capt. Frank Dicello. He and I had become good friends, and as his unit was part of the II Field Force general court-martial jurisdiction, he prosecuted their courts-martial and I defended.

We tried the case from early morning until late at night, determined to finish in a few days. The witnesses testified from photographs of the bunker in question. The bunker was against a wall, the usual sandbags, revetment, and heavy beams. Beyond the wall, the ubiquitous palm trees. On the roof of the bunker, some folding chairs.

The prosecution witnesses testified that on November 5, shortly before nine in the evening, one Sergeant Buchanan, the squad leader, and five members of the squad were sitting on top of the bunker, visiting. It was a warm, clear night, with a full moon. Since it was almost time to sleep, the men began to discuss guard duty for the night.

Specialist Urquhart accused Gomez of having slept on guard the night before. Gomez called Urquhart a "mother fucker." Soon Gomez and Urquhart were fighting, and continued until separated. Gomez then took a knife from his pocket and advanced on Urquhart, the blade exposed and shining in the moonlight. Urquhart grabbed a cot and held it up between himself and the knife until Sergeant Buchanan took the knife away from Gomez and told him he should fight with his fists like a man. The fight continued until Gomez said he had had enough and climbed down from the top of the bunker and went inside to the sleeping area.

There was a moment of calm until Sergeant Buchanan called down from the top of the bunker and told Gomez that he

would stand first relief guard for that night. Gomez then came
out of the hooch with his M-16 rifle in his hand. Sergeant
Buchanan grabbed the M-16 rifle lying on top of the bunker and
stood up on the cot and said if anybody was going to do any
shooting he would be the one to do it. Gomez asked Buchanan if
he wanted to die, and Buchanan said, "No."

Burchanan got off the cot, threw the weapon down on the
cot, and began walking away from Gomez, saying, "If you are
going to shoot me, go ahead." Gomez placed a magazine in his
weapon, chambered a round, said, "I'm going to shoot you,"
and fired two or three short bursts on automatic, striking
Buchanan in the hip and buttock region of the left side of the
upper part of the back of the left leg. Urquhart saw that
Buchanan had been hit, and the other witnesses testified that
Buchanan yelled out and Gomez said, "Say it again and I'll
shoot you in the head." Gomez then fired another burst from
his weapon.

As a result of the shooting Sergeant Buchanan had suffered
injuries to the left sciatic nerve, a fracture of the right and left
trochanter, and a fracture of the left ilium. Since the sciatic
nerve courses down the inside back of the thigh and into the
buttock region, and since the trochanter is the lateral hipbone,
and since the ilium is the flaring bone at the extremity of the
hip, it was apparent that the sergeant had been severely injured.

The prosecution rested, and I put on Gomez. I knew he had
his own story to tell, but I wanted it to come from him and not
from me, so I had made the decision not to make an opening
statement. He was soft-spoken with a slight Spanish accent. He
had an engaging way of cocking his head slightly to the left and
smiling faintly when listening to the question. He knew he had a
lot at risk, and he was determined to be a good, respectful
witness.

Q: What, if anything, happened when you got to the bunker?
A: When I got to the bunker Specialist Urquhart came over to
     where I was and started an argument with me which led
     me into a scuffle. I remember him beating me and banging

my head against the wall and later he laid me on the cot
and was hitting me. I managed to push Specialist Urquhart
away from me and I got in a crouch position and shoved
him away from me. I noticed that he lifted a cot that was
there against the machine gun position and I reached in my
pocket and pulled out a knife trying to scare him away
from me because I had told him I didn't want to fight anymore. Then Specialist Urquhart pushed the cot toward me
and I lifted my arm up to shove the cot away. I noticed that
Sergeant Buchanan came in between us and told me to give
him the knife and grabbed me by my left hand. . . .

Q: And what happened next?
A: When I saw Sergeant Buchanan with the weapon I heard
     him pull the bolt back on the weapon and I reacted auto-
     matically the same way. I turned around to see if anybody
     else was armed because I thought they were all against me.
     At this time I heard a click from where Sergeant Buchanan
     was and by instinct I turned around and I fired low. I never
     intended to hurt Sergeant Buchanan.

Q: What did you intend to do?
A: I was trying to throw him off balance because I was afraid
     he was going to shoot me.

The president of the court then asked a question: he wanted
to know where Sergeant Buchanan was. This posed a problem.
Sergeant Buchanan was still in the hospital in San Francisco. I
knew that it would hurt Gomez if the court knew how badly
Buchanan was injured. During the side bar conference the law
officer, the prosecutor, and I agreed to enter into a stipulation
that Buchanan was in the United States and was not available.
Would any civilian prosecutor or judge have been so scrupulous
in avoiding prejudice to the defendant?

After arguments, the colonel gave instructions as to the
law. It was early evening when the court went into deliberation,
and after a few hours they returned with their verdict. In
civilian courts, or even in military courts in peacetime, two
hours is considered to be a very short deliberation: in Vietnam,
it was about as long as you could expect the officers to devote to
the case.

Gomez and I approached the court, saluted the president of the court (always the highest ranking officer who acted as jury foreman), and stood at attention:

PRESIDENT: Sp4c Samuel Gomez, it is my duty as president of this court to inform you that the court in closed session upon secret written ballot, two-thirds of the members present at the time the vote was taken concurring in each of the findings of guilty finds you:

Of the Specification of the Charge: Guilty, except for the words, "with intent to commit murder" and the words "by shooting him with an M-16 rifle" and substituting for the latter phrase the words "by shooting him with a dangerous weapon, to wit, an M-16 rifle." Of the excepted words, not guilty. Of the substituted words, guilty.

Of the charge: Not guilty, but guilty of a violation of Article 128.

Of the Specification of the Additional Charge: Guilty except for the words "by cutting at him with a dangerous weapon, a means likely to produce grievous bodily harm, to wit, a knife" and substituting therefore the words "by striking at him with a knife." Of the excepted words, not guilty. Of the substituted words, guilty.

He had been found innocent of his charges, but guilty of lesser included offenses. We were running ahead. Now it was time to continue before the same court in the same matter, for sentencing. I had a few witnesses and used them quickly. The court wanted to hear from Gomez. They looked sympathetic, and I knew the best way to keep their sympathy would be to move as quickly as possible. I put Gomez on, and he told about his family.

Q: Now you state that you're not married but you have a contribution to family. Who are you contributing to?

A: I'm helping my parents out and my sister who's going to college.

Q: What is the condition of your father in regard to employment:

A: My father has been ill. When I left for Vietnam he was in the hospital. He has trouble with his legs and has sugar diabetes. He started drinking quite heavily when I left for Vietnam and at this time he is unemployed.

Then I began to read the letters. I had written away for letters and had received them from his parents, from a justice of the peace in his town, from his former high school counselor, from the president of the school board, from his neighbors, from a teacher in vocational training (bringing out his former presidency of the Future Farmers of America), and I ran through them quickly and handed them to the president of the court.

The court was tired, and my gut instinct was to let the officers rule now. They had worked hard, and they were anxious to get back to their units. Their helicopters were waiting on our helipad and they had other matters to concern themselves with. They would not take it kindly if I were the cause of their having to wait another day. I argued for Sam, and they went back to the screened-in back porch of our courtroom, overlooking the bunkers and across the road to widow's village, and they made their decision.

Sp4c Gomez, it is my duty as president of this court to inform you that the court in closed session and upon secret written ballot, two-thirds of the members present at the time the vote was taken concurring, sentence you:

To forfeiture all pay and allowances, to be confined at hard labor for twelve months, and to be discharged from the service with a bad conduct discharge, and to be reduced to the grade of E-1.

So Sam Gomez went off to Leavenworth, the officers went back to their home units, and Frank Dicello and I went off to find a friendly ice cube and a little gin and tonic. Two friendly adversaries, blanking out the day's work, neither asking, "What do you suppose really happened?" Neither caring.

I remember many other cases in which I was either defense counsel, or prosecutor, or peripherally involved in one way or another. When I first came to Vietnam, the stockade riot cases were being tried. There had been a serious riot at the USARV Installation Stockade, and some of the men involved had been prosecuted. With almost admirable ingenuity, the filters of cigarettes had been stuffed into the locks on cells and set afire; of course that had led to the rule against filter cigarettes in the stockade. I remember watching one case in which the defendant testified that he had not, in fact, been rioting but had been seeking to avoid the rioters and had wandered into the mess hall, where he had calmly sat down and eaten a cake. He had further testified that at the time he was under the influence of binoctol, or "French sleeping pills" as he called them. In retrospect, his testimony had a certain eerie humor to it. And there was an exhausted humor of sorts in our daily law practice, along with much that was depressing or merely bizarre. I remember once I had gone out to Redcatcher, perhaps to interview a witness, and a snake had crawled into the partition between two offices. We had taken sticks and boards and killed it, then we tried to get somebody to tell us whether or not it was one of the sixty varieties of poisonous snake in Vietnam. For no reason at all, we decided to name the dead snake "Cheap Charlie," and we filled out a military assistance card for it. I suppose we were keeping statistics at the time. We reached hard to find humor wherever we could.

Much that happened to us was merely exasperating. Once I was anxious to get out of Tay Ninh, partly because we had been hit there the night before, but mostly because I needed to have a scheduled rabies shot stuck into my belly the next morning. I could not catch a chopper out, as they were all full. I finally somewhat timidly approached what appeared to be a commercial airplane parked on the helipad. I stuck my nose in, and a cheerful red-faced Air Force colonel invited me in, told me I could ride along to Saigon with him, and instructed the Vietnamese steward to bring me a bottle of orange soda. It turned out that one of his friends was having a going-away party in Saigon that night, so an airplane had been sent to pick him up. I flew back with him to Saigon's major helipad (Hotel 3) and caught a chopper from there to Redcarpet which was home.

Winning cases don't get typed up; the government cannot appeal. And perhaps there are other, personal reasons why I tend to forget my acquittals and to remember my losses. But there are cases that, for one reason or another, hover at the edge of my memory.

For instance, there was the night two young soldiers had just seen the John Wayne "Green Beret" movie. One soldier pointed an M-16 at a friend and said, "I'm John Wayne." His buddy responded by raising a captured AK-47 and saying, "No, I am"—and then, meaning no harm, chopping his buddy in half with automatic fire. And I have very vague recollections of whorehouse shootings, or minor cases involving the sale of "repacks"—American cigarette packages in which the final inch of each cigarette had been replaced with marijuana and the altered cigarettes had been repacked—nineteen to a package —and sold on post.

I had always wanted to visit Cam Ranh Bay, and I finally got my chance when Bob Jones loaned me out to defend a sergeant major charged with assault with a rifle. The sergeant major had worked for a Capt. Pierre di Vincentes, himself a lawyer, though Pierre was assigned to a medical service position, rather than judge advocate.

Pierre put me up at his BOQ, cooked lobster in an excellent Italian sauce, and entertained me royally. The case itself came down to two young black GIs taking over the day room, their black sergeant major ordering them out, their calling him an Oreo cookie (black on the outside, white on the inside), and their advancing on him in a menacing way. He fired a warning shot, then shot one of the men in the arm.

After I had investigated the case, I became convinced I could get a dismissal without going to trial. We took a jeep up to Nha Trang to see the convening authority. I told the colonel that the two young soldiers were clearly acting in violation of

Article 94 of the Uniform Code of Military Justice—under which any person who acts in concert with any other person to "usurp or override lawful military authority . . ." or refuses in concert with another person "to obey orders or otherwise to do his duty or creates any violence or disturbance . . ." was guilty of mutiny. I explained that the offense of mutiny was punishable by death or "such other punishment as a court-martial may direct," and that the death penalty was also applicable to anybody who was found guilty of "failure to suppress" a mutiny. In other words, the two young soldiers, by taking over the orderly room and acting in concert with one another, were guilty of mutiny. Had my client failed to stop or prevent their unlawful acts, he would also have been guilty under Article 94. Clearly he had both the right and the duty to end the unlawful activity. I sat there, feeling quite smug and pleased with myself.

The colonel, a soft-spoken man of little humor, looked me right in the eye and told me he would agree to dismiss the charges—on the condition that I prosecute the wounded mutineer! I argued that the gunshot had been punishment enough, but the colonel kept me on the hook—so I prosecuted the "victim" in a special court-martial, got a conviction, and did not resist defense counsel's requests regarding sentencing.

Cam Ranh remains a kind of paradise among my Vietnam memories. Once Pierre borrowed (somehow) a general's launch, and we went yachting one Sunday afternoon to a nearby friendly island. Another time we sailed on a small, clean inland lake—enjoying every moment of the sandy beaches and the recreation. Then, back on a C-130 to Bien Hoa, and a hitchhiked jeep ride back to the Plantation, wondering what mission Bob Jones had waiting for me.

There were cases in which we simply did the best we could, and some of our work, in retrospect, seems idiotic. I once defended a cook who was charged with fragging. He was of Hungarian descent, and as a boy had fled Hungary during the anti-Communist uprising. He testified that he had seen his father killed by a Russian firing squad; and the court was with him. But then I had to get smart and call some witnesses to testify to the effect that once during the rocket attack my client's primary concern had been that his pies not burn in the oven, and somehow my closing argument wandered off into the area of the importance of good food for a functioning army. Perhaps I was hungry, or merely exhausted, but the court apparently did not hold it against either me or my client.

We did the best we could with what we had, and my extensive travels in connection with cases large and small had given me the confidence and know-how I would need for the Green Beret case.

Long Binh, South Vietnam. Six Green Beret officers, facing an Army trial on charges of murder and conspiracy in the death of a Vietnamese double agent, talk with military defense counsel, Capt. John S. Berry, right. From the left: Capt. Budge Williams, Maj. Thomas C. Middleton (hidden), Capt. Leland J. Brumley, Capt. Robert F. Marasco, Maj. David E. Crew, Col. Robert D. Rheault and Berry. (Lefthand corner: Bob Rheault.)

Thumbs up for freed Green Berets, outside their barracks at Long Binh base. From left: Capt. John S. Berry, his client Capt. Leland J. Brumley, Maj. Thomas C. Middleton, and Capt. Robert F. Marasco.

PART THREE

Those Gallant Men

After such knowledge, what forgiveness? Think now
History has many cunning passages, contrived corridors
And issues . . .
. . . .
. . . Think

Neither fear nor courage saves us. Unnatural vices
Are fathered by our heroism. Virtues
Are forced upon us by our impudent crimes.

—T. S. Eliot, "Gerontion"

WHO HAD BEEN RESPONSIBLE FOR SALARIO'S *death? How had the net been compromised? Slowly, painstakingly, the captains pored over their files. Convinced that the leaks must have come from a Vietnamese national, they went over the files again and again, reducing the suspects to a mere half dozen. One of the captains yawned, stretched, said, "To hell with it. I'm getting some coffee."*

Another, tired, discouraged, abandoned his files and began sorting new data, laying each paper neatly across the steel desk. Suddenly he was on his feet. "Jesus Christ!" he roared. "Here it is!" The other two captains crowded around the desk. There was the photograph, and unmistakably . . .

"Get him in. Get him in for questioning. Now." The major was excited but cautious. He wanted no mistakes. There must be no more leaks, no more deaths caused by security leaks. "But," he admonished his men, "be certain. Don't go tying a can on some innocent man."

Days later, a captain and a major sat at the same steel desk. "It's certain. The polygraph, the sodium pentothal, and everything else falls into place."

The major leaned back. "Army coffee," he sighed. "It'll kill you." He thumbed through the file again. "Let's go to Saigon. Find out what the Agency wants to do with him." He paused. "Maybe they can give him sanctuary somewhere, until we are certain he can't do any more damage. We can't keep him around here anymore."

The major began pacing. "I hope they don't suggest . . ." He stopped, sat back at the desk. "It's an Agency operation; it'll be an Agency solution."

Later, in a jeep, one captain turned to another.

"Can you believe those assholes? They don't say 'kill.' They say 'terminate with extreme prejudice.' Cute, huh. I don't like shooting anybody who can't shoot back. And anyway, what's this crap about filling him with morphine first? Is that supposed to make it merciful?"

"Nah." The other captain field stripped his cigarette.

"That's to make him bleed more, so the sharks will get to him faster."

In every lawsuit, even those protected by a secret classification, there are uncontroverted facts that become part of the public record and are undeniable. There is no doubt that a Vietnamese national named Thai Khac Chuyen disappeared on or about June 20, 1969. Nor is there any doubt that Col. Robert Rheault, commander of the 5th Special Forces Group, was charged with his murder, and that if convicted he would face a mandatory sentence of death or life imprisonment. And there is no doubt that some of his officers, including Maj. David Crew, Maj. Thomas Middleton, Capt. Leland Brumley, Capt. Robert Marasco, Capt. Budge Williams, and CWO Edward Boyle were all similarly charged. As if it were not enough that these officers be charged with premeditated murder, they were each also charged with conspiring "from 15 June 1969 to 20 June 1969" to murder the same Thai Khac Chuyen, whom the prosecution erroneously called Chuyen Thai Khac. The second charge also carried a penalty of life imprisonment.

My own involvement in the case was the result of Lt. Col. Robert Jones's willingness to "loan" me out to other units, whenever there was a shortage of counsel in a case he believed I would enjoy. In this case, he was puzzled and told me that he had not been told the name of my defendant or the nature of the charge. Only that it was a "murder" case, and that I could have it if I wanted it. Because the jeep and my driver were immediately available, I left for Long Binh and USARV headquarters. I was still puzzled when I reported to Colonel Rector, the deputy staff judge advocate for USARV, under Col. Wilton Persons.

Colonel Rector was crisp and formal. I put him slightly on edge by commenting on how much I enjoyed coming to Long Binh, with the flush toilets, the air-conditioned offices, and the attractive personnel. I am certain that Rector was an excellent officer, but there was never a very good chemistry between us. "Captain Berry, you will report to the USARV Installation Stockade. Your client's name is Capt. Leland Brumley, but even that fact is classified secret. When you get to the gate of the stockade, you will not mention Brumley's name. You will ask for Number Six. You will not discuss his name, or the charges against him, or the fact that you are representing him with anybody.''

I shrugged my shoulders and wandered out of his office, wondering if perhaps he hadn't been a little more dramatic than necessary. After all, a murder case was just a murder case. Or at least that was what I thought at the beginning.

At the Long Binh Jail, I first met Capt. Leland Brumley. I never wore my uniform very well—my clients occasionally commented on my frayed shirts with unbuttoned pockets, my scuffed boots, which I could never quite manage to blouse without having bootlaces dragging behind me—and there was no doubt in my mind that I appeared unmilitary to him. Anybody observing my generally rumpled appearance and his very soldierlike bearing, would have thought I had been the one who had spent the night locked up in solitary confinement in a steel CONEX box, and that he had been the one who had just left a comfortable office.

We sat together and visited awhile before we began to discuss the case. He was reluctant to trust me at first. We began to visit a little bit about our general backgrounds. Leland was trim, obviously athletic. He had black hair and dark eyes, and the natural caution of a combat intelligence officer. I was anxious to get as much background as I could from him, about the specifics of his murder charge and the covert and clandestine operation it arose from; my trial lawyer instincts and experience directed my inquiry to the relationship between the Special Forces and the CIA. I had been in-country long enough to know that there was some kind of working relationship between the two organizations at a top-secret level, and the secrecy with which this case was being handled alerted me to the significance of that issue. It was common knowledge in the military that since the Bay of Pigs fiasco, the CIA had learned to rely on others such as the Special Forces for information-gathering purposes. I had an immediate suspicion that Brumley might be in the dangerous position of being used as a scapegoat for a CIA snafu of some kind.

But Brumley was cautious, and during our initial conversations, I told him as much about myself as I thought might interest him and asked him about his personal background. There was not much else he was willing to discuss with me at that time.

Lee Brumley was twenty-seven years old. Born, raised, and educated in Oklahoma, he had been an Eagle Scout as a boy and had always loved the out-of-doors. He was graduated from the University of Oklahoma and entered the army in January 1965. After completing the infantry officer school at Fort Benning, Georgia (four years after I had completed the same school), he went to airborne school and qualified for the jump badge. From there he had taken a military intelligence course at Fort Holabird, Maryland, and then took additional schooling at Fort Bragg, North Carolina. Finally, he was sent to Vietnam at the end of 1965.

During his first assignment in Vietnam, he had been with the 173d Airborne Brigade, which at the time was known as Westmoreland's favorite. He had a year of more or less constant combat experience during that twelve-month tour. Although he had always been interested in military intelligence, his tour with the 173d had brought his concern for good intelligence gathering to a level of personal obsession. He was convinced that the North Vietnamese Army and the Viet Cong fought only when they chose to fight and in circumstances that were favorable to them. He knew that when the American intelligence was good enough to be able to force a fight on American terms, America had a very high degree of success. But because the North Vietnamese and the Viet Cong seemed to have a very real edge in terms of intelligence, most real combat found the American troops outnumbered. The North Vietnamese and Viet Cong were able to concentrate in masses and strike vulnerable points, even when the American forces were conducting multiunit sweeps. Lee Brumley had left convinced that American training, numbers, and weapons meant absolutely nothing without better intelligence.

So at the end of his tour he requested the six-month counterintelligence course at Fort Holabird. There he studied offensive and defensive counterintelligence operations and learned the techniques of preventing effective enemy intelligence penetration. The central point of Brumley's training was that enemy agent penetration was the prime intelligence disaster; an emergency to be dealt with. Brumley studied case histories of successful German and Soviet penetrations of the British intelligence services, and the resulting capture and death of British and American agents. Lee Brumley and his fellow students learned of the catastrophic example of Kim Philby, who had come so very close to destroying MI-6, an intelligence fiasco from which the British Intelligence Services have never completely recovered. Brumley's interest in military intelligence grew steadily stronger, and his desire to get back to Vietnam to use his new skills became urgent. He took additional courses in tradecraft, including the use of intelligence photography, the making of microdots, and other aspects of intelligence work.

Despite his requests to be reassigned to Vietnam, he was first assigned to Fort Sill, Oklahoma, where he was the commander of a counterintelligence unit. Much of his work at that time was still classified top secret, and Lee had headed up the successful investigation of a clandestine group of men who were secretly attempting disruption of the army from within the army. That operation sharpened Lee Brumley's skills as far as recruitment, training, use of double agents, and photography.

There was one other delay that kept Lee Brumley from getting back to combat. He was assigned to a nine-month intelligence career course. That nine months expanded and deepened his intelligence skills, and when he finally got his orders to return to Vietnam, he felt fully prepared to practice his intelligence specialty in a tactical situation. He specifically requested Special Forces, because he knew of the relationship between the

5th Special Forces Group and the CIA, and he understood the importance of the Special Forces in intelligence gathering in Vietnam. His job in Vietnam had been chief of counterintelligence with the American Special Forces Group. His section had been busy conducting operations against both the North Vietnamese Army and our allies, the South Vietnamese.

After we discussed all of that, I sensed a real hesitancy on Brumley's part to give me much more information. Lee had explained to me that the Green Berets, all the way from northern I Corps to the southern Delta, had a number of teams working with Vietnamese. Much of what the 5th Special Forces did was done in connection with the Civilian Irregular Defense Group Program, which was generally referred to as CIDG. There were approximately eighty installations from the DMZ to the Gulf of Siam, most of which were manned by at least an A Team of American Special Forces soldiers (two officers and ten men) and had a jack leg battalion of Vietnamese—many of whom were Montagnards, Cao Dai, Hoa Hao, or some other religious or ethnic minority group of Vietnamese, who worked with the Americans. He explained that there were numerous installations and training centers, and that there were B Teams to run logistical and operational headquarters, in addition to numerous special organizations dedicated to the training of Vietnamese. Each group had its own installation and its own intelligence and its own security to manage. Each camp had its own group of Vietnamese agents who were used specifically for counterintelligence. So at the time Chuyen had disappeared, the Green Berets in Vietnam had between four thousand and forty-five hundred Americans, and perhaps forty thousand to forty-five thousand indigenous troops spread across the country.

Brumley began to explain some of B-57 to me. I understood by now that Chuyen had been an agent for B-57. I knew that many of the Green Beret operations in Vietnam were bilateral in the sense that intelligence was shared with our Vietnamese allies. But, Brumley told me, B-57 was unilateral. B-57 purported to be a civil affairs unit, but its actual mission—and the intelligence it gathered—was not shared with our Vietnamese allies.

Brumley abruptly shifted the conversation into the general area of military law procedures and the status of his confinement. He told me that if they had had to lock him in a tiny steel box, they could have at least arranged one that would keep the rain out! And he began to joke, mildly, about the fact that he should be getting double combat pay for being an Oklahoman with his life in a Nebraskan's hands . . . and we exchanged some regional humor. He further was amused by the fact that his single-edged razor blade had been taken away from him, and he had been given instead a razor that had in it a seven-inch steel band, with which, he assured me, anybody with any training at all could escape from that box and handle the guards if he so chose.

I finally left, knowing that he did not completely trust me and was not about to open up to me, either as to the charges against him or the nature of his military operations. It struck me that he had probably been lied to very recently, during his CID interrogation, and that he was wary of being fooled again. So I did not press. It is not uncommon that the details of any case come out slowly and over a period of time. It would have been unusual if he had given me a full disclosure as to everything involved in the Chuyen operation, that first time we visited.

Because of his caution toward me, I simply gave him the usual admonitions against speaking to anybody, told him a little bit about the time-honored prosecution tactic of planting "buddies" to get defendants to talk, and told him that since this was a conspiracy case, it might be a very good idea for me to work closely with the other defense counsel. He talked about his wife and young daughter, and I shook his hand and left. Later, he told me that I had seemed shocked by his incarceration and by his being charged with murder.

Before I left the stockade, I decided that the first thing I would do would be to violate Colonel Rector's order against talking about the case. Leland Brumley was charged with conspiracy to commit murder. I would immediately find out who was representing the other defendants, so that we could work together for our clients. After all, Captain Brumley was entitled to effective assistance of counsel; no consideration of national security was going to prevent him from getting that.

Every defense lawyer has his own intelligence-gathering apparatus, and it was not long before I learned the names of two other defense counsel: Maj. Marty Linsky and Capt. Bill Hart. Both were stationed at the huge Long Binh base, and I found them immediately and persuaded them to take a drive with me, away from their offices. Marty Linsky was a tough New York kid. He had attended Fordham Law School and had a reputation as an excellent, slashing advocate. He had already completed his military service obligation but had extended for an additional six months, for the opportunity of serving in Vietnam. His manner of speech was quick, aggressive, and occasionally cutting—in contrast to the exaggerated country drawl of Bill Hart, who was a red-headed Idaho boy, known for his gentle sense of humor and his passionate courtroom appeals, both of which masked a very practical, problem-solving approach to the law.

We found a secluded spot near some storage tanks, and I told my driver to take a walk. The three of us sat in the jeep, and as we began to piece the case together, we realized that Col. Robert B. Rheault, commander of the Green Berets in Vietnam, was being charged, along with a handful of officers, with conspiring to murder a Vietnamese double agent.

We sat together, and I gave them my theory of the case: we must work together; by working together we could probably get acquittals for everybody; God help us all if any deals were made. I went back to my office, and Colonel Rector called me and asked me if my client would like to bargain for immunity, by disclosing the location of the body. My answer was "What body?" That was the last time I talked plea bargain in the case.

Despite the admonitions of secrecy, Marty, Bill, and I worked together to plan our defense as best we could in the time available. We would soon be at the preliminary hearing (usually called the Article 32 hearing in the military), and it was our fervent hope that, at that hearing, we could keep the matter from going to trial. Perhaps we could keep Colonel Persons from writing a pretrial advice recommending trial on the charges. We would not only defend our clients, but in the process we would prevent what we were beginning to understand would become the destruction of the 5th Special Forces Group.

II

If the prosecution had been genuinely concerned about national security, there was an obvious solution: dismiss the case! This was the position the Green Beret defense must take, even though the army had quite literal control over our very lives. (We would do no more or less than insist on a valid constitutional right. The intensity of our advocacy in so doing should not be confused with "disruption advocacy," which has to do with directly attacking orderly courtroom procedure. We were out to preserve the constitution, not destroy it.)

Our motives in working together lay partly in the complex nature of the law of criminal conspiracy. At common law, a criminal conspiracy is an agreement between two or more persons to accomplish together a criminal or an unlawful act, or to achieve *by criminal means* an act not in itself criminal or unlawful. Also, there has to be an overt act in furtherance of the agreement. The "overt act" might not be criminal in nature. And the agreement in itself is not a crime.

During a trial, if prima facie proof of conspiracy is shown, acts or declarations of one conspirator are admissible into evidence against any other member of the conspiracy, *even if the other accused coconspirator knew nothing about those acts at the time they were done.* The courts relax the hearsay rule, and a defendant being tried for conspiracy may be convicted on hearsay, if that hearsay consists of a statement "made by one in furtherance of the conspiracy."

Under the Uniform Code of Military Justice as it was in effect at that time, conspiracy under Article 81 appeared to follow the general conspiracy laws everywhere. The military law was that each conspirator would be liable for all of the acts of the other members of the conspiracy done in furtherance of the conspiracy during its existence, and that a person could be guilty of conspiracy although incapable himself of committing the intended offense. The elements of proof of conspiracy under the Code were that the accused and one or more other persons named or described entered an agreement; that the object of the agreement was to commit an offense under the Code; and that one or more of the persons named or described performed an act to effect the object of the conspiracy. The "overt act," in and of itself, did not need to be criminal. It merely needed to be a "manifestation that the conspiracy was being executed." Under the table of maximum punishments, a person found guilty of conspiracy would be subject to the maximum punishment authorized for the offense which was the object of the conspiracy, except that the death penalty could not be imposed merely for conspiracy. So our defendants would be facing a possible death penalty for the murder charge and a possible life sentence for the conspiracy charge.

Although the laws vary from jurisdiction to jurisdiction, a general rule of thumb is that in a conspiracy case, it is to the prosecution's advantage to encourage personal disloyalty among the defendants, so as to fragment the defense. But these were not men to whom betrayal was possible.

III

One reporter had referred to the CIA/Green Beret relationship as "an incestuous marriage between the sneaky Petes and the spooks." Until 1964, the Central Intelligence Agency had been in control of the United States Special Forces in Vietnam. In 1964, in an operation known as "Parasol/Switchback," the Agency relinquished control to the military. Until that time, all

Special Forces programs had been funded by the CIA. It may have been the Bay of Pigs fiasco that had begun the policy of the CIA moving away from operations as such. Although the Agency remained an important and powerful intelligence-gathering organization, military operations were turned over to the army. Still, there continued to be advantages to transferring Department of Defense funds to the CIA, so that various programs could operate under CIA rules rather than the more restrictive military regulations.

By 1966, intelligence gathering had become the only connection between the Special Forces and the CIA. In 1966, the 5th Special Forces Group rewrote its basic intelligence operations to conform with the rest of the intelligence community. This placed the director of the CIA in the chain of command. The members of the 5th Special Forces Group were responsible to their own officers, and nobody in the CIA had the authority to give any Green Beret any orders, except from the very top. The CIA in Vietnam functioned largely to receive Special Forces intelligence.

During my visits with Brumley, and my conferences with Linsky and Hart, I discovered that Rheault had never met most of his codefendants. He dealt directly with Maj. Tom Middleton, who was Group S-2 (Intelligence) and was the principal staff operator officer to report on intelligence to Rheault. Maj. David Crew was the commander of B-57, and he, like Middleton, reported to a Colonel Facey, who was Rheault's deputy. Middleton had staff responsibility for Crew's operation and these two dealt with Rheault, while Leland Brumley, as chief of counterintelligence reported directly to Middleton. At the time they were charged with murder and conspiracy to commit murder, Rheault had never met Leland Brumley, nor had he ever met a number of the other intelligence officers who were made defendants—Budge Williams, Bob Marasco, and Eddie Boyle were people whom Colonel Rheault would see for the first time in a courtroom, while being charged with conspiring with them to commit murder.

B-57 had been created to establish agent networks in those Special Forces camps that would operate across the Vietnamese border into Cambodia and sometimes Laos. Our ally, the Republic of Vietnam, was not supposed to know of its existence, even though B-57, to succeed, had to use South Vietnamese employees. Because America, by crossing the border into Cambodia and Laos, was in violation of treaties with those countries as well as South Vietnam, there was a general policy against American "grey ghosts" actually crossing the borders.

By the spring of 1969, B-57 was probably one of our most successful secret operations. Most commanders in the field felt that these intelligence-gathering missions, though "illegal," had saved numerous American and South Vietnamese lives. It had begun to appear that Leland Brumley's dream would come true — that America would be able to fight a war in which American intelligence prevailed. His intelligence work against the North Vietnamese and the Viet Cong was so successful that by April of 1969 he and the people with whom he was working were intercepting information from the NVA-VC Courier Service. Through such intelligence, the Green Berets had eliminated a highly effective enemy intelligence reconnaissance unit operating from the islands off Nha Trang Bay and from the mountains south of the city.

And Brumley had done extensive work in operations to stop the graft and corruption of our Vietnamese allies, and especially the LLDB (Vietnamese Special Forces). This included the selling of weapons and medical supplies to the North Vietnamese Army and the murder of their own troops for threat of exposure. The LLDB had some excellent and heroic individual members; however, it was generally reputed to be the most corrupt of all ARVN units. Brumley's operation was moving along well, with witnesses in safe houses, and the exposure of the criminal activities at the very top of the Vietnamese Special Forces was imminent.

Then, at about the same time, important sources were killed, dried up, or simply disappeared. The evidence began to mount that our nets were being compromised. The Special Forces Group found itself in a situation in which its entire information-gathering apparatus was severely threatened. Lives would be lost either through the compromising of our secret missions, or through our failure to get necessary intelligence, or through the deliberate feeding of misinformation through double agents. Brumley and the men he worked with were determined to find the leak, and when they found the double agent, they would seek to have the CIA put him where he would be unable to communicate with our South Vietnamese allies. He had been working day and night on his various projects, and the compromising of the B-57 nets through a double agent was just one of the many problems that filled his days. And, he wryly reminded me, at least part of his time and energy went to fighting a war.

Capt. Bob Marasco was a fairly recent transfer to B-57. As with Brumley, he was not Special Forces qualified, but rather was an airborne army officer assigned to the Special Forces Group. That was fairly common in B-57, and Marasco had been in military intelligence with the 101st Airborne Division and was assigned to B-57 as a team leader. A B-57 team was not a traditional Special Forces A Team (twelve to fourteen men) but consisted only of three or four men at a time. The team was in charge of a camp based in the Delta. Their apparent job was to advise the Vietnamese in the Special Forces camp, but in reality the men from the team exercised much greater authority, in terms of operations, supplies, and administration.

The top-secret Cambodian bombing had begun, and B-57 was sending back map overlays from the area to aid the Air Force in targeting enemy installations. Some of these overlays were obtained by indigenous personnel, both Cambodian and Vietnamese, recruited and trained by B-57, who operated under the cover of selling food to the VC/NVA units in Cambodia. The information they gathered was transmitted by clandestine radio, or by a secret courier system, to sources who then transmitted it directly to the White House. Bombing attacks were planned, based on the overlays and other intelligence gathered by agents working for B-57. But Marasco had been complaining that his net was drying up.

IV

During the period of time we were awaiting the hearing itself, Marty, Bill, and I pooled the knowledge we acquired from our clients, who were kept isolated from one another. I formed very clear pictures of men I had never met: Rheault, Marasco, and of course Budge Williams, who was, to me, among the most interesting and enjoyable of the defendants.

It was Capt. Budge Williams who brought Leland Brumley the damning photographs of Chuyen. Budge was a likable cross between a Special Forces "snake eater" and a "good old boy." Budge was born and raised in Georgia and attended the University of Georgia. After graduation, he went into the army with gusto: Airborne School, Ranger School, Special Forces School at Fort Bragg, Jungle Training School in Panama. Unlike most of the other defendants, who were not originally Special Forces trained but rather were attached for intelligence purposes, Budge started out with the idea of being in Special Forces.

He had also attended military intelligence school and originally went to Vietnam with the 135th Military Intelligence Attachment. His first assignment was to a field office at Duc Hoa, a small village between Saigon and Cambodia. There he set up "resident offices" in four provinces, and after his year's tour of duty he voluntarily extended and was assigned to the 5th Special Forces Group, where his duty was that of a group collection officer in S-2 (Intelligence), coordinating clandestine activities, primarily in Cambodia and Laos.

After six months in that assignment, he was transferred to the Canal Zone, and the 8th Special Forces Group, again in a military intelligence detachment. After about a year, he went back to the 5th Special Forces Group in Vietnam and was assigned to B-57 when another captain was convicted of shooting a double agent. In 1968, B-57 was operating out of Saigon under the cover of being a civic action unit.

Budge told me that he had crossed over into Cambodia on several occasions, working with Vietnamese nationals. Normally Americans did not cross over into Cambodia but operated there through our allied agents. Crossing the border, other than in hot pursuit of Viet Cong forces, was dangerous, partly because we had no method within our system to recover Americans once they got into Cambodia, and partly because the discovered presence of an American might well have "blown" our missions there. So Budge had tried to stay on the Vietnamese side of the border whenever possible. But he had been involved in reconnaissance and interception of communications by wire taps on telephone cables, and in other forms of intelligence gathering. He had always gone over "sterile" with no American equipment. It was his custom to use foreign weapons, foreign radios, and false identification papers.

The Vietnamese who worked for B-57 were not Vietnamese Special Forces, and the Vietnamese government did not receive any of the B-57 intelligence. Budge had long thought that the real reason for the unilateral nature of the operation was for the protection of our own agents. The Vietnamese Special Forces had a Mafia-like reputation for shaking down intelligence agents for their salary, and forcing them into compromising situations, and feeding them false intelligence. When Marasco had arrived from the 101st Airborne Division, Williams was the operations officer for B-57. Williams had never met Brumley or his assistant, WO Eddie Boyle. While it was Williams's duty to gather intelligence, Brumley and Boyle as counterintelligence officers were concerned with security investigations, polygraphs, and other methods to keep enemy intelligence at bay. It was not unusual that Brumley and Williams would not have met; B-57 was spread out in a dozen camps along the Cambodian border, and there were many people involved in the operation who had never met one another.

As operations officer for B-57, Williams had become an

expert in gathering and sorting information. On a daily basis, there were codes to be broken, messages to be transferred, and reports to be hand carried to Saigon within twenty-four hours of completion.

Williams had become alarmed by the decline in the information he received from the Marasco team. At first he believed that Marasco, being new to the job, might simply be short on experience, but later it became apparent that Marasco himself was receiving bad intelligence. The other B-57 teams had been sending useful information, but nothing of any value was coming from the Marasco team.

Williams met Marasco, became convinced of Marasco's competence, and developed a strong suspicion that there was a double agent somewhere involved in B-57. It was while Williams was mulling over the problems with that team, that one of his sergeants found the photographs of Chuyen with North Vietnamese officers. The photographs had been discovered in an abandoned American camp northeast of Ban Me Thuot in the Central Highlands, used by the North Vietnamese Army as a staging area for some years. A 3d Mobile Strike Force Operation had recently attacked the camp and had captured many documents, including rolls of film of the North Vietnamese Army unit participating in political and indoctrination activities. Chuyen was in many of the photographs, sometimes by himself and other times with high-ranking NVA officers. Williams took the photographs to Brumley who by now also realized that the problems throughout B-57 had been even greater than Williams had known. Brumley knew he was looking for a double agent, even before he had the photographs. Williams, upon further investigation, discovered that Chuyen had previously been "terminated with prejudice" (fired, not subject to being rehired) by another Special Forces unit for suspicious activities, yet there had been no mention of this in his dossier.

In the meantime, Marasco had been on R & R. When he returned, Brumley, Crew, and Williams were all suspicious of Chuyen, and Marasco positively identified Chuyen as being the same soldier who was photographed with the North Vietnamese officers.

Brumley sent Marasco out to his field station and instructed him to tell Chuyen that he was being considered for an important mission. Brumley was convinced that if Chuyen was in fact the leak and the double agent, that he was very good, indeed, to have escaped detection for so long. Brumley also decided to send his very best polygraph operator along with an agent to Saigon to have them interrogate Chuyen and conduct a polygraph examination. The polygraph operator reported back to Brumley that there was absolutely no doubt that Chuyen was a double agent and was the leak that had led to the compromising and drying up of nets.

Brumley then ordered that Chuyen be secretly moved to an airfield, where he would be flown in a small civilian twin engine plane belonging to the CIA to Nha Trang and made as comfortable as possible pending further interrogation by Eddie Boyle and Brumley. He was again questioned and polygraphed, and was given sodium Pentothal on a controlled basis, but was not at any time tortured. The captured photographs, the results of the polygraph examination, the results of the interrogation under sodium Pentothal, and the results of other background information gathered about Chuyen, combined with the problems that had arisen in connection with operations in which Chuyen had acted as interpreter, convinced the seasoned intelligence and counterintelligence officers that Chuyen actually was the double agent.

There could be no doubt that Chuyen had caused dangerous breaches in security, and that his release would lead to even more serious security problems. Since the CIA was the logical recipient of this intelligence, and since the CIA was (at the very top at any rate) in the chain of command, the obvious solution was for some of the officers to report to the CIA headquarters in Saigon for further instructions.

Crew and Williams went to the embassy building in Saigon to meet with the CIA assistant station chief. The station chief in

Saigon was not present at the time. They suggested to the CIA that the Agency provide a place where Chuyen could be incarcerated so that he could give out no more information. It was certain that, if turned over to the South Vietnamese, he would be tortured by them and would tell them whatever he knew. On the other hand, there was no doubt that, if released, he would pass on whatever information he had to the Viet Cong and the North Vietnamese.

Amid the plush offices on the sixth floor of the embassy, Crew and Williams visited with men whom they had never seen before and whose very names they suspected of being false. There was good furniture, thick carpeting, and attractive American women working as secretaries. Williams thought he was back at the Pentagon. Crew persisted in questioning about the possibility of an island where Chuyen could be kept in restriction at least long enough for a good assessment to be made of the damage he had already done.

The nameless, faceless men in the embassy building instructed Crew and Brumley to get rid of the man. Not satisfied, Crew and Williams then went to another CIA office in Nha Trang.

V

Col. Robert Rheault had recently become the commander of the 5th Special Forces Group. He was trim, austere, and a clear product of West Point. Rheault had been the commander of the 1st Special Forces Group in Okinawa before taking his new command in Vietnam. Bob Rheault was a man whose principal motivation was that of working with our Vietnamese allies, in ways that would most make them self-sufficient. He had believed that by close cooperation with the South Vietnamese, they could be assisted in defending themselves, and eventually would be able to determine their own form of government. He had no illusions about the likelihood of the Viet Cong or North Vietnamese ever allowing a democratic government to exist in the South.

Whatever forces had stirred the case up in the beginning, there were deep-seated rivalries and angers within the army that now came to bear on the situation. Gen. Creighton Abrams was an old tanker. Because of the excellent performance by armor during the Second World War, he was firmly convinced that it was the destiny of the armor branch to control the army. But then came the "airborne Mafia"; Taylor, Ridgway, Westmoreland, and others, and the Green Berets, who represented an elite fighting force—a concept that seemed to offend Abrams. There had already been one bad incident between Rheault and Abrams. In 1969, there was talk of troop withdrawal, and there had been some suggestions that perhaps the 5th Special Forces Group, since they had been the first unit to come into Vietnam, should be the first unit to go home. Rheault visited Abrams and expressed his professional opinion that the group should be the last unit to leave; that they should be allowed to remain in the country until it was certain that the Vietnamese Army could, in its own way, defend itself and South Vietnam from the North. Rheault had mentioned that if there were to be a reduction of forces, the reduction should come from the fat, rather than the muscle. He had bit his tongue and had refrained from suggesting that it would be more appropriate to send home the white-jacketed waiters from General Abrams's mess than the 5th Special Forces Group. He did mention that the Special Forces were the only American presence in many areas in Vietnam, and stressed that if there was to be a phaseout, it should be done in an intelligent way. When he had finished his speech, Abrams had simply glared at him, asked "Are you finished now, Colonel?" and Rheault had saluted and left.

Abrams was, to many people, a fair and honorable old soldier. But he would have been superhuman not to have let his resentment toward the Special Forces concept interfere with and influence his decisions in the Green Beret case.

Men from the CID began "dropping in" on the Special Forces headquarters at Nha Trang. One by one, Major Middleton, Major Crew, Captain Marasco, and others were suddenly missing from camp. This happened while Rheault was out in the field. Since Rheault was newly arrived in Vietnam in his current command, he was anxious to make his presence felt. He had made a showing of throwing out the queen-sized bed his predecessor had used and installing a simple army cot. He went out to the field, and, as a commander of a group that at the time consisted of almost forty-five hundred Americans and perhaps forty-five thousand indigenous troops spread out across the entire country in approximately eighty installations, he had a great deal on his mind besides the operations of B-57.

Rheault had always been interested in working with the indigenous Vietnamese. In a previous tour, he had been initiated into a Montagnard tribe. He dealt directly with some thirty tribes strung up and down the mountain chain. Not only were these people America's strongest allies, but Rheault found himself in deep sympathy with them. The original inhabitants of Vietnam before the Sino-Mongoloid invasion, they had been driven out of the best areas in Vietnam, their treatment being similar to that of the native American Indians in North America. During the year 1964–65, Rheault had been the executive officer for operations among the Special Forces in Vietnam, and had found that his linguistic ability had come in handy.

Rheault had spent the previous five years concerning himself with unconventional warfare activities. As with Brumley, he believed intelligence to be the secret of success in any war. He knew it was crucial that American soldiers understand the political nature of the war. Clearly, there were many Vietnamese migrating from North Vietnam to South Vietnam to escape an oppressive regime. Clearly, the South offered greater freedoms of the right to dissent, as well as the availability of newspapers and education. Yet, as Rheault was fond of saying, "You could kill guerrillas all day long and they would spring up like dragon's teeth."

Rheault was determined to find and work at the root causes of guerrilla warfare. No matter that the guerrillas were supported externally, the fact was that there were guerrillas, and they were dedicated to their cause. He preached to his men that the indiscriminate burning of a village with five Viet Cong in it was not only immoral and illegal but was poor soldiering—there would now be five hundred new Viet Cong recruits from the angered people. So Rheault was concerned with matters far beyond the scope of an isolated double agent, or how that double agent was disposed of. The CID agents knew that, and they further knew that he could be counted on to be out in the boondocks, away from his men. So they came and, one at a time, gathered the suspect officers in.

Brumley's intelligence duties were staggering. In addition to his other chores, he was concerned about the welfare of his men. At this particular time he had received some disturbing news: Sfc. Alvin Smith had gone to the CIA to ask for "sanctuary." Apparently, Smith, who had been involved in the Chuyen investigation, had concluded that Brumley and the other officers were acting in a cool and secretive manner toward him. Smith had become afraid and had gone to the CIA's Nha Trang office for safety. His reasons, or motives, for so doing were beyond Brumley's imaginings. But he had other matters with which to concern himself. Criminal Investigation was sending an agent up to inquire about a "sensitive matter" within the Special Forces Group.

When the CID agents approached Leland Brumley, he was getting ready to exercise. He often found relaxation in running and was irritated by their interruption. They told him that they intended to interrogate Boyle (who had assisted Brumley in his investigation of the Chuyen matter). They "asked" Brumley to help them find Boyle, so Lee spent the evening leading them around Nha Trang where he knew Boyle would not be. He thought he should visit with Boyle before they did.

Eventually, Boyle and Marasco were taken out of the field, then Crew disappeared, then Middleton. So there was no surprise when, in a day or two, the CID agents asked Williams and Brumley to go with them to Saigon. Brumley was instructed to bring with him a .22 automatic Colt Woodsman with a silencer, if he had one. His unit did have such a weapon and he brought it with him though, as far as he knew, it had nothing to do with anything the CID might be investigating.

When Budge Williams and Lee Brumley were apprehended, Williams had been expecting it. He had his rucksack packed and was, as he put it, "like a chicken in a cage waiting to be fried." Williams had been living in a two-story wooden barracks that housed several hundred soldiers, most of them Montagnards. He had joked that living above the Montagnards, who cooked and ate food "that would make a damn alligator throw up," had prepared him for whatever could happen.

The CID agents flew Williams and Brumley to Long Binh where they were put up in an old two-story Southeast Asian hut. The agents had told Williams and Brumley that they should plan to be gone only for "a couple of days." At the empty safe house where they were taken, Williams napped, and when he awoke he saw that Brumley had already been removed. Williams was then taken to a trailer in Long Binh where Brumley, Marasco, and Boyle were being held. The CID agents assured him that if he would answer their questions "everything would blow over," and he would be sent back to his unit and his job.

Instead, however, he and the other men were taken to the Long Binh Jail where they were searched. The MPs found hand grenades in Williams's rucksack. They were locked into tiny cells where there was not enough room to stretch out full length on the floor. The daily rains poured in from a large opening in the roof. CID interrogations continued. The cells were separated so that the men were isolated from one another. The guards were clearly perplexed as to the circumstances of the arrest and incarceration. One of them asked Williams if he had been a part of a plot to overthrow the American government or assassinate the President.

Rheault had always thought of the Special Forces as a very elite and special group. When he returned to Nha Trang and discovered that his men had been spirited away without his knowledge or consent, he flew to Long Binh in a rage. He went directly to General Mabry, who was the commander of the

United States Army in Vietnam (subordinate of course to Abrams, who commanded all of the branches). Rheault stood at attention before Mabry.

Rheault with his close-cropped graying hair, his deep tan, his starched jungle fatigues with combat infantry badge and master jump insignia, his Montagnard bracelet—perhaps the thin Philippine cigar between his teeth (if he was invited to sit), and the combination of forces that had shaped his personality came to bear on the instant. Rheault was a man with graduate degrees from Georgetown and the University of Paris, and his combat experiences were somehow interwoven with his tour as an assistant professor of foreign languages at West Point—a complex man, inscrutable in his way. Rheault has a very real sense of humor, but I doubt that his warmth and humor showed at that meeting. He must have been pure steel. He looked Mabry in the eye and cooly demanded that either his men be released, or that he, as commander of the Green Berets in Vietnam, be charged with murder and imprisoned. Mabry ordered Rheault imprisoned. Rheault, who had just flown down from Nha Trang, dutifully surrendered his sidearm and jungle knife and submitted to arrest and confinement. He had made his decision to stand trial with his men.

Mabry was not about to cross General Abrams, and the command's advice would come from Col. Wilton Persons, a fellow classmate of Rheault in the West Point class of 1946. Persons had been Rheault's friend and, in fact, earlier had borrowed Rheault's house and boats at Martha's Vineyard. But this was to become a lawsuit of grave importance, and neither Bob Rheault nor any other defendant could possibly have predicted which side of the issues his various friends and acquaintances would adopt; Bob Rheault would soon find that courtrooms were the locus of a different kind of warfare.

VI

Our Article 32 hearing was set for July 31. For reasons of

secrecy, the command had scheduled it to be held in the stockade chapel. As with the rest of the compound, the atmosphere was equal parts heat, disinfectant, and despair. And as with the rest of the case, the hearing began on a note that underscored the prosecution's insistence on secrecy, and the power and determination of our adversary.

At the outset, Colonel Sieman, the investigating officer who would initially recommend whether or not the defendants should be bound over for trial, introduced a certain captain, who was the Assistant Chief of Staff G-2 (Intelligence) for Headquarters, USARV. Since the entire hearing was classified secret, the captain was there to make certain that the required nondisclosure statements were completed. He informed us that the statements were "a mere formality for this court," explaining that classified material should not be divulged outside of the court or hearing.

I was the first defense counsel to speak, and I took my position: "Regarding the security briefing on behalf of my client . . . I want to make it clear at the outset that by signing this certificate I don't intend in any way to waive our right to public trial guaranteed by the Sixth Amendment or waive our right to consult or employ civilian defense counsel. And further, in our signing this, nothing herein shall be interpreted as a waiver of our vigorous defense of this case as provided for by the Constitution, and I want to be on record as saying this, sir, in case the issue should ever come up."

All other military defense counsel immediately joined in my statement.

I did not want the army to get the idea that they were going to get away with secrecy in this case. My opening words in the case established our theme throughout.

My small speech marked the first time Rheault, Crew, Williams, Marasco, Boyle, and Middleton had heard my voice. Except for Rheault, the men had been locked up separately in the Long Binh Jail, living in little steel boxes under the murderous sun, and no communication between them had been allowed. A mutual process of acquaintanceship was now in progress. Even Sgt. Alvin Smith, the man whose visit to the CIA office had instigated the charges against him and his codefendants, must have felt a kind of wistful camaraderie, since in many respects his rights were being protected by lawyers who were representing men he had, in fact, reported. I confess to having felt a certain sympathy for Sergeant Smith, though I was careful never to express that to my client.

The defendants and their lawyers were seated in parallel lines of tables, facing one another. Both were perpendicular to the tables at the end of the room where the investigating officer, the prosecuting attorneys, the court reporter, and the witnesses sat. There was nothing else in that room, except a tall upright fan that was not up to the task of circulating the very hot air. From the outside, we could hear sounds of the Long Binh Jail—custody officers managing their prisoners and occasional work details. All of us, both defense and prosecution, were wiping our hands on the trouser legs of our jungle fatigues so that at least our hands would be dry enough not to blot the ubiquitous yellow sheets on which we were to make notes. The government was pleading secrecy, but of course the separation of the men, and their inability to work together in their own defense, struck me as being a little too consistent with Ltc. Rector's earlier orders that would have kept defense counsel away from one another. So I immediately made another small speech to the effect that my client was being denied effective assistance of counsel and that "it is impossible to properly prepare for this hearing while being in confinement . . ." under the existing conditions. We did not expect immediate results, but we were determined to change the nature of the pretrial confinement.

Colonel Sieman's job was becoming more complicated than he had thought it was going to be. And we intended to make it a whole lot more complicated. In a way, I had to sympathize with him. He had, after all, been appointed to render an impartial decision, but he had been appointed by people who served over him, and who had made the decision to proceed with the charges. Additionally, his experience, if any, in previous Article 32 hearings must have been with the short, quick, preliminary hearings so favored by prosecutors the world over.

In any lawsuit, the party with the burden of proof will attempt to keep the issues narrow. Defense counsel will use the preliminary hearing for discovery purposes, and the broader he can make the issues, the more he is likely to find out—and the more difficult it will be for the prosecution to satisfy the magistrate that the case is there. So when Colonel Sieman began with the pro forma statement that the defendants had the right to present anything they might desire on their own behalf, I was ready, and on my feet.

I told him we wanted ". . . the Bravo 57 case file containing, but not limited to, the intelligence reports of the alleged victim, any contracts of the alleged victim, a name trace report on the alleged victim, an operations interest report on the alleged victim . . . testimony of Brigadier General Potts who is the G-2 at MACV; Major General Thomsen, Chief of Staff, . . . a complete list of all agents at Moc Hoa that are in any way affiliated with Bravo 57 or the CIA. Also, sir, a complete list of all agents in Than Tri. . . . In addition, sir, I would like a passenger list of all the people who came from North Vietnam on the Mirabelle in 1954, and a complete report as to the NVA or VC affiliation of any and all of these people."

We wanted to leave no doubt that we had certain facts at our disposal and were prepared to use them. I continued: ". . . I would like a complete list of any memos that have passed between the CIA and the CID regarding the case now under investigation. I would also like available from the Vietnamese government any files by military security surveillance regarding the alleged victim."

I further requested ". . . a dossier on the alleged victim, any dossier on him and any member of his family, including his sister who works for MACCORD, . . . any messages from Nha Trang to Saigon or from Saigon to Nha Trang regarding the case file . . . the CIA messages, sir, regarding the CIA or CID, regarding any operations regarding the alleged victim. Sir, we request any statements made, any statements, record statements made to the CID by the same Colonel ——— or Captain ——— and Colonel ———, the same individuals who have already been requested. We request the presence, sir, of Mr. ———, the ——— worker at ———. . . .

"Sir, we request the operational plan of Than Tri Cypress regarding Bravo 57. We request the Operational Plan Blackbeard. Sir, we request all terminations with extreme prejudice in unilateral operations since 1961. Similarly we request a list of all terminations with extreme prejudice in bilateral operations since 1961, and similarly we would request a list of all terminations with extreme prejudice in multilateral operations since 1961, and including especially the Provisional Recon Unit."

He still wanted to know what I was talking about and I went on: "Sir, termination with extreme prejudice has to do with various methods of getting rid of agents who have outlived their usefulness, and we request a list of all instances in which that has been done here in Vietnam since 1961 by the United States or allies. This information should be available from the CIA.

"Additionally, from the 5th Special Forces, the polygraph office operators . . ." The prosecution could do nothing but wait for us to make our record; we had come out swinging.

Finally, the prosecution got a chance to call their first witness, a Colonel Facey, who had been the deputy commander of the 5th Special Forces Group under Colonel Rheault. Facey, being second in command, had worked closely with Rheault and obviously admired him. He looked drawn as he took the oath. His face was pale, his fists clenched as he testified generally about attending some meetings "concerning a compromise of a certain agent from the depth of B-57 operations." He said he had attended meetings regarding a "possible security problem with reference to a possible penetration of a clandestine operation from which the 5th Group had USARV responsibility."

He stated that one of the defendants had said "that he had reason to believe that one of the agents that was hired or employed by Detachment B-57 for clandestine intelligence operations was, in fact, a VC who had penetrated the operation." He testified that among the discussions of how to deal with the agent, "one was that the agent should be continued to be employed on isolated, closely guarded missions, his future conduct to be observed. Number two, the agent could be dismissed from the program. Number three, the agent should be eliminated."

These discussions were "mostly dealing with the impact that it would have on B-57 intelligence operations if, in fact, a VC agent had penetrated it." He said subsequently, "There was indication to me about two possibilities; one was the possibility that the plan had been carried out, and it was also an indication that the agent was sent on a mission."

The witness was, in his way, typical of the prosecution witnesses in that case. He was torn against himself. He wanted to be a good soldier but also wanted to be an honorable man. His desire to be loyal to his comrades on the one hand and to fulfill the wishes of the command on the other had him in a state of anguish. Under other circumstances I would have liked the man. Colonel Facey had no knowledge of any killing, or any plan to kill, or any agreement to do so. He was a "background" witness and had done us no real harm. In an actual trial, I might have waived cross-examination entirely. But this was a preliminary hearing, and I was there to get educated.

My cross-examination was brief and to the point. I made it a matter of record that the witness appeared with his own lawyer, who was sitting next to him and was conferring with him from time to time. Then I set out to show if Chuyen had in fact been executed, that his death was necessary and fully in accord with the customs of warfare in force and effect at that time, and in that place.

Q: You say Bravo 57 has to do with our unilateral operations in Cambodia, is that correct?
A: Yes, sir.

Q: And in an earlier statement did you not say that due to the unilateral nature of the operation, that the open disclosure of such would undoubtedly cause international problems?

A: I made that statement.

Q: Can you tell us why the open disclosure of Bravo 57 would cause international problems?

A: Primarily because we were operating unilaterally, U.S. intelligence operations, from this sovereign nation of Vietnam without consulting—into the country of Cambodia without their knowledge.

Q: Would it be correct to say then, that it was considered to be in the interest of the United States that the government of Vietnam not know that we were conducting unilateral operations into Cambodia?

A: I would make an assumption that is why it became a unilateral operation to begin with. They didn't want them to know.

Q: Do you know whether or not it is unusual to discuss the possibility of eliminating an agent?

A: In the business or the field of intelligence it is not unusual to discuss this.

Q: Sir, when an agent is eliminated, is it usually considered to be a military necessity to eliminate him?

A: In my opinion, yes.

The execution of double agents is one of the tragic unanswerable issues of war. It is clearly permissible to kill a uniformed enemy with whom one is engaged in combat. Of course, it is clearly not permissible to kill civilians or those members of the enemy who have surrendered. What precisely are the rules regarding spies and double agents? Anybody who has seen very many movies, or read very many spy books, will operate on the assumption that the normal and proper procedure is to simply eliminate them. One imagines a James Bond movie, in which Bond ends up facing trial for murder, perhaps with M being charged with conspiracy to commit murder.

Q: Sir, would it be correct to say that if the CIA knew that man was going to be eliminated and they did not in fact

preempt, this would be a form of a go-ahead by the CIA as
a practical matter?

A: To the best of my belief I would say, yes, it would be a full
go-ahead.

Under my examination the witness identified Black Beard
as the code name for B-57 intelligence operations into Cambodia. He further testified that if Chuyen were allowed to compromise B-57's mission, and even if that compromise did not
result in the deaths of members of the net, it would render the
net ineffective "in addition to placing the United States in an
unfavorable light." When I asked him if General Abrams himself had not approved of the nets and their results, he answered,
"I sat next to COMUSMACV when he made that statement." It
always delighted me when Abrams was referred to simply as
COMUSMACV (Commander of the United States Military
Assistance Command in Vietnam)—somehow reminiscent of
the papacy.

After I had finished with the witness, Bill Hart examined,
showing that "the longer you held the agent, the more pre-
carious the situation became," and he got the witness to agree
that "something had to be done." Hart was followed by a Captain Booth, Middleton's lawyer, whose questions established
that "the operations of the 5th Special Forces Group were in
fact working for CIA," and Booth further wanted to know the
probable results of the Vietnamese or Cambodian governments
learning about the operations. Colonel Facey said that "if the
government of Vietnam were aware of the fact that we were
conducting clandestine intelligence operations from within
their territory into Cambodia, they may damn well be very
upset about it. . . ." Then Linsky used his cross-examination to
pin down the fact that this witness was never present at any
meeting at which any decision regarding Chuyen was reached.

After all defense counsel had cross-examined the witness,
Capt. Roger Nixt of the prosecution team had an opportunity to
conduct redirect examination. Nixt was a good personal friend,

and both of us had grown up in rural Iowa. Our friendship would be tested by this hearing but would survive it. Roger could sense that the thrust of the defense case had legal merits, and rather than evade the issue, as the command subsequently attempted to do, he rose to meet it.

> Q: Do you know for a fact, or only suspect, that this agent was in fact a double agent?
> A: I suspect.

Of course I had to come back with further questions on recross-examination.

> Q: Isn't it a fact that most of the intelligence work — it is something less than absolute certain knowledge — you do the best you can with what you have available. Isn't that generally how you have to operate?
> A: Yes.

I wanted the hearing officer and whoever else read the record to know that we were dealing with the real, brutal world of counterintelligence during warfare!

> Q: Isn't it also true that under sodium Pentothal, certain information got out that indicated he was NVA or VC? Isn't it a fact that the suspicion, as Captain Nixt uses the term, was based in part on the results of the test under sodium Pentothal and extensive interrogation with and without sodium Pentothal?
> A: This is what has been told.

I drove on, using the government's witness to make our case. The "victim" was a spy, and by God the prosecution wasn't going to get away with denying it!

> Q: Isn't it also true that this suspicion had to do with some compromises in some nets that this individual had been involved in?
> A: This is also what I have been told.

Q: Isn't this suspicion also brought up by some photographs in
      which this photograph of a known VC agent was seen to be
      the same as the alleged victim is, sir?
A: Yes, sir.

Now, just in case anybody had missed the point, I pounded
in the last nail: "Sir, based on this, would you say that this was
something stronger than mere suspicion that he might be a VC
agent?"

In credit to Colonel Facey, he responded to my sarcasm
with courtesy: "In my opinion, they had a basis for being concerned about the individual, yes."

A witness may be called on direct examination and may be
cross-examined. Redirect examination is usually used to reha-
bilitate the witness and to rescue his testimony from whatever
damage has been done on cross. Recross-examination is used to
discredit the rehabilitation that has been achieved during
redirect. Then there is re-redirect . . .

Colonel Facey generally testified to the military necessity
of the nets that were in existence and had been compromised.
He testified to the CIA funding for Green Beret activities, and to
the fact that when Black Beard went across the Cambodian border, the equipment carried could not be regular U.S. Army
equipment but rather had to be sanitized, since it was not being
used on official American missions. He testified about the
"country team" concepts, in which the team consists of the
ambassador, representatives from the military, representatives
from AID, CIA, and others, in all countries in which we had
diplomatic missions. He testified that General Abrams was the
military representative to the ambassador in the country team
we had in place in Vietnam at that time.

In any murder case, there is a certain amount of nervous-
ness at the outset. The first witness grounds the case in reality,
and the tension gives way to hard, careful work. There are those
who describe the trial of a murder case as being similar to
"jumping from building to building with a live baby in your

arms—on television." But by the time we had finished with Colonel Facey, we on the defense team were relaxed and enjoying ourselves. And, I found, I was beginning a friendship with each of the defendants. An appreciative nod, a raised eyebrow, a wry scowl or a shrug—these men who had heretofore been hypothetical codefendants were emerging as compelling individuals. Although Rheault sat as a defendant, it was impossible not to believe that it was he who was in command and control of the proceedings. And the time we defense counsel had spent together in preparation was paying off—we were working as a team.

The prosecution began calling witnesses involved with supply. One testified that "Captain Brumley said that he would need clearance from the Binh Tam boat launcher area, out through the south river, to the area of Bich Dam, which is located on Hon Tre Island. . . ."

His basic testimony was that the men had wanted a boat on June 20, stated that they would want it again the next evening, that they took the boat out again the next evening, that one of the men had stated that the boat would be washed, that when the boat was tipped, he could observe that the water was tinted red, and that it was "common knowledge that there was being held in the B-57 area a Vietnamese agent about whom there had been some suspicions." Another sergeant was brought in and was asked to stand guard in the hallway to keep anyone from entering the building during the specified time "that the agent Chuyen was supposed to be removed from the building."

There was a supply sergeant then called to testify that one of the officers had requested to borrow a silencer for an M-16. Then a captain was called to testify that one of the officers had requested twenty-five feet of link chain.

There are very few lawsuits that are won or lost by one statement or one sudden dramatic gesture. The more complicated the case is, the more isolated bits of evidence are needed to be set forth in some kind of sequence for the purpose of laying foundation for additional bits of evidence, which, added together, may or may not prove the case. It is impossible to imagine the effects a lawsuit has on people who come within its sphere. In the Green Beret case, this ripple effect was increased by the knowledge of the various witnesses that the outcome of the case could affect their military careers, or even the date when they could go home.

The case erupted into one of the many controversies that characterized it throughout. Colonel Persons had informed the defense counsel that a certain Major Kane under his command was to be made available to all defense counsel as the "super defense counsel." That same Major Kane now appeared as the attorney for a prosecution witness, who had specifically requested other counsel. I first thought that the prosecution had (ironically) planted a "double agent" among us. Kane, our super defense counsel, and now attorney for a prosecution witness, would (months later) represent the command at a Pentagon hearing investigating the manner in which the Green Beret case had been handled at the command level.

I made a record that I had told the super defense counsel what my strategy was going to be. The entire adversary system is predicated on the idea that the defense and the prosecution will be opposed to one another, and therefore separate from one another. When the prosecution begins hovering a little too closely around the defense, of course the defendant is deprived of his right to assistance of counsel. Colonel Persons's apparent planting of one of the prosecution counsel looked suspicious in light of Colonel Rector's initial orders to defense counsel not to talk with one another. Marty Linsky has since convinced me that these were merely a series of coincidences and that it is not unusual, in the army, for a lawyer to move back and forth among defense and prosecution functions. At the time, however, I was inclined toward suspicion of Persons, Kane, and Rector.

The witness whom Kane represented was a Sergeant Ishimoto. He testified that on June 20 he was placed on guard in the

B-57 headquarters and was told not to let anybody into detachment headquarters. Further, that he saw someone in a litter being placed into an ambulance, and that the next morning he traveled by aircraft to Tay Ninh.

The investigating officer asked, "Did you presume you were going to the Tay Ninh area for assignment or for a mission or what?"

Ishimoto answered: "I didn't presume anything, sir; I was given an order. I have faith in my leaders and I follow that order." He testified that his aircraft did arrive in Tay Ninh, that he was met at the airfield by two captains and taken to a field team, and later went to B-32, which is in Tay Ninh, stayed overnight, and left the next morning for Saigon.

I had immediately liked this witness, and although he was called by the prosecution to try to establish a cover-up, there was no doubt in my mind that he would be absolutely honest. The prosecution theory was that Ishimoto, being of Oriental descent and having worn tiger fatigues, was ordered to pose as Chuyen who, according to the government's theory, had already been murdered. I saw my cross-examination as an opportunity to attack a forthcoming witness:

Q: Sergeant Ishimoto, you initially made your statement to Mr. ———, didn't you?
A: Yes, sir.
Q: And to get you to make this statement, he made certain promises to you, didn't he?
A: Yes, sir.
Q: And will you tell us what those promises were?
A: Sir, I was told at the time I made the statement that at any time in the future I could see General Abrams concerning this matter.
Q: You didn't realize at the time that ——— was lying, did you?
A: No, sir.
Q: When did you find out ——— was lying?
A: This morning, sir.

The CID agent whose credibility I had attacked through Sergeant Ishimoto testified after lunch. I wanted to find out from him the extent to which that other agency, the CIA, was involved in the case.

Q: Is the CIA involved in this investigation in any way?
A: Sir?
Q: The CIA?
A: Yes, sir, I believe they are.
Q: What instructions did you receive from the CIA, if any?
A: Sir, I wouldn't classify them as instructions. I attended a meeting. I would have to look up the exact date. A Mr. ——— from the CIA was at the meeting. He read four or five reasons why his people would not be permitted to be interviewed in the course of my investigation.
Q: So then, from the exalted offices of the CIA, your position was going to be, if there was a scapegoat, it could only be military; it couldn't be anybody from the CIA?
A: All I know is where the line was drawn.
Q: It is the halls of the CIA to which this investigation has not reached, is that correct?
A: Yes, sir, that's correct.

I specifically questioned him as to whether or not, in any of the meetings involving generals, any general had seemed concerned with the fact that the CIA was going to get away with whatever had happened—that the army was going to be taking all the blame for the CIA. I asked if any of the generals had been at all bothered by that fact.

A: Sir, I don't know what goes on in generals' minds. I know they didn't say anything. . . .
Q: And were they all pretty much agreed that it would be a pretty good thing to avoid a public trial?
A: . . . I could say that probably if I were in their shoes, I would prefer it not to be a public trial. I am sure that this is the way they felt. You had better ask them.
Q: Unfortunately, I don't have them here, but you can rest assured that I am going to try to get all of them here.
A: Yes, sir.

Direct, cross, redirect, recross, questions continued. The afternoon wore on, tempers were lost and regained, voices were raised and grew hoarse. A stack of papers was handed out to defense counsel with the suggestion that we examine them and determine if there were any additional individuals we would like to call as witnesses. My exhausted statement was as follows: "Frankly, receiving these at 1800 hours, my brain is so dull and fatigued and exhausted that I really can't come up with an intelligent analysis of this at all. I will be honest, I am trying to read it and if I see anything, I will let you know."

After adjournment, defense counsel gathered together for a drink and some heavy planning. We were convinced that we were entitled to all of the top-secret information we had requested. Since *Brady* v *Maryland*, the law has been that the government may not withhold exculpatory evidence if the defense requests it. Trials were to be a quest for the truth, and it would be unfair for the government to conceal requested information crucial to the defense. The prosecution has virtually unlimited funds, and the prosecution gets into a case before defense counsel even knows a case exists. In this case the government had a ton of classified information, and we wanted and needed it, and, in our youthful idealism, were convinced that we would get it.

Bill Hart clapped my back. "We got 'em running, buddy. No way the government's going to want this one to come to trial." Marty Linsky was pensive: "I don't know if you guys recognized them, but there were a bunch of reporters—AP and UPI—hanging around outside the gate. If any word of this gets out, the government will have their backs to the wall, and they won't be able to dismiss if they want to." I shrugged. "So who's going to tell them?" We went back to the Long Binh Jail.

But when we reconvened on August 2, the case exploded on us. Colonel Sieman refused most of our requests for additional witnesses. Although some would be called, we would be denied others, including the man who had run the polygraph examination of Chuyen. I was first stunned, then enraged. I was on my feet, and Marty Linsky later claimed that my voice shook the steel walls of our hearing room: ". . . if ever it is established that anybody was killed . . . the guilt or innocence of these men may well hinge on . . . the total environment, the total flow of circumstances . . . instructions, customs of warfare, military necessity. . . . I would personally like to have the privilege of forcing each and every one of these . . . witnesses to state what he refuses to testify to on the grounds of executive immunity."

Colonel Sieman listened courteously, but I was getting nowhere. Still, the court reporter was taking it all down, and I wanted to make certain that President Nixon and General Abrams (and there was no doubt, even then, that Nixon would make the final decision on the case) understood the scope of the case. I began to discuss my cross-examination of the CID witness: ". . . I tried to ask him was there any indication anywhere by any of the generals that perhaps army loyalty should run downhill as well as uphill. . . . The army was to be sacrificed in the interests of the CIA. I asked him was there one spark of courage. Was there any indication anywhere that loyalty and justice were at least as important as another star . . . this record is morally offensive . . . a colossal whitewashing, something just short of a conspiracy on a very high level. We have some people here who are to be sacrificed. . . . A whitewash is a vicious unconstitutional thing."

I had not been impressed with the explanation that we were denied the CID report because it was not yet completed: ". . . we would like . . . every scrap of paper they have . . . those pieces of paper that show that Chuyen was a VC/NVA agent . . ."

I had warmed up to my main point, and now I made it: *"If the government wishes to keep all of this secret, it may not try my client. The government has a choice. It may bring forth everything . . . and try my client, in which case we will gladly go to court, or it can drop the charges against my client. The government may not do both, sir."* I had vented my rage, and I had made my record. Nothing was going to change here. Now it was time to get out of there and regroup. I said, "Sir, . . . we have reached the point at which . . . none of our clients can be properly represented . . . unless they have civilian counsel. . . . We have run into . . . an unconstitutional brick wall." Defense counsel jointly moved for a continuance and walked out.

Hart and Linsky were angry but not discouraged. We needed a lawyer who would be vigorous, learned, fearless, and who would resist the temptation to bring the press in on the case. I had previously met Henry Rothblatt at a trial lawyers' seminar in Las Vegas, and I had used his textbooks and form books. The other lawyers agreed with my choice of Henry, and I wrote him, careful to note "privileged and confidential" on the outside of the envelope and to write my name over the seal, then to cover my signature and the seal with scotch tape. We were more than a little paranoid about our case, but with good reason, as it turned out. Henry must have been shocked that we were asking him to leave his very lucrative New York practice, to fly to Vietnam at his own expense, and to represent some very good men in a very bad case, with no possibility of ever receiving a fee. So I threw in the hook: "This case will be unique in legal history, Mr. Rothblatt, and I promise you that if you do come, your skills and talents will be taxed to their utmost."

Rothblatt agreed to come, but before he arrived, another civilian defense counsel had done damage that, at the time, seemed irreparable. Tom Middleton had written to an old friend, a Mr. Gregory of South Carolina. Gregory apparently decided that the proper way to become involved in a criminal conspiracy trial would be to hold press conferences with national media, before even interviewing his client. One suspects that Mr. Gregory may be a highly competent general practitioner in his own community. But as he held his press conferences wherever his plane stopped (including Hawaii) on his way to Vietnam, he effectively destroyed our hopes of getting an early dismissal. He left the prosecution nowhere to go but forward—and did so without ever visiting with his client or with Dick Booth, who was Tom Middleton's very competent military defense counsel. Gregory managed to get his own picture in *Time*

Magazine and, reporters later told me, met with the press in Saigon and suggested that Chuyen himself might appear at the trial as a defense witness!

Hart, Linsky, and I joined with the other defense counsel in trying to salvage what we could. Our clients were still in the steel CONEX boxes, and we visited them when we could. Although the men were still locked up in isolation in their five-by-seven-foot steel boxes, taking their daily meals handed in slots under the door, they had managed a system of communication among them in the Long Binh Jail. Lee Brumley filled his days with pushups and plans. When we visited, it was usually about the case, though he would still find time for a wry remark.

There was an air of urgency in all that we did. We had been granted a three-week continuance between the first half of the preliminary hearing and the last half, and we all tried to get our other work up to date. There were still wills to be written, cases to be disposed of, soldierly duties to be attended to—and carefully worded letters home. Since Gregory had blown the whistle, we were generally referred to as defense counsel for the case, and even if we had wanted to forget the case, we could not have done so. Every soldier I met felt somehow involved in the case, or at least touched by it.

One grunt asked me if I could meet briefly to explain to his squad "which ones you can kill and which ones you can't." Again and again we were approached by men asking what they could do to help us. Even in Saigon we got some special attention. Somebody had taken a picture of the defense team, and it had appeared in several of the twenty or so Vietnamese-language newspapers that flourished in Saigon in those days.

It was time to reassess our relationship with the press. If it had been discreet to avoid them before, there might now be some value in cultivating them. Still, it was an uneasy relationship. Most of the reporters I knew were delighted with our willingness to stand up against the command. Our chief point of disagreement was that while I was beginning to understand their cynicism toward Abrams, none of them seemed to share my skepticism about the North Vietnamese and the Viet Cong. When I suggested, for instance, that an American withdrawal from Vietnam would probably spell an end to the press freedoms enjoyed by both the Vietnamese and foreign journalists (including Americans), my statements were greeted with hoots of derision. I would get along just fine with the press if I would keep my comments within the very narrow range of the Green Beret case. And on that subject, I said very little.

VII

On August 18, Marty, Bill and I took a jeep to Tan Son Nhut to pick up Henry Rothblatt. We hustled him off to the Caravelle Hotel, where he freshened up, ordered lots of food and drink, placed his books in strategic positions around the room, and invited the press up to talk with us. He was, as I knew he would be, pure velvet. The reporters and correspondents thumbed through several of the texts he had coauthored with F. Lee Bailey, appeared to enjoy the treats Henry had graciously provided for them, and scanned his curriculum vitae. They were fresh from their recent sessions with Gregory, so Henry was careful to establish his credentials and tried to quell some of the hysteria Gregory had fomented. "I am here to inject reason on *both* sides of the issue," Henry crooned. Marty Linsky winked at me. Henry just might pull it off.

We had told Henry that Mr. Gregory was going to make any settlement impossible. We told him where Gregory was living, and Henry excused himself for a few hours. He came back and assured us that we would have no more trouble with Gregory. We spent the next day taking Henry from tailor shop to tailor shop, where he had Vietnamese walking suits made for himself, suitable and appropriate for the tropical heat. And of course he bought some Vietnamese paintings, had some portraits made of himself, and enjoyed being in the war zone. But it was time to get Henry back to the Plantation, to brief him on the case, and to get ready for the impending hearing.

My boss, Lt. Col. Bob Jones, had arranged for Henry to stay in an air-conditioned trailer at the Plantation. Bob made certain Henry was issued a set of jungle fatigues, and he even got Henry invited to dinner at the general's mess—and made certain I got to come along, too. Years later, Rothblatt would still speak of Jones's gracious hospitality—making a fellow lawyer feel at home.

On August 20, we were back in court. At first Henry had not been allowed to take the record of the previous hearing out of the USARV offices to study it. But our motion to get the men out of the stockade and into a more agreeable confinement situation had been suddenly (on Henry's arrival) granted. The defendants now were moved to a small barracks at Long Binh, where they were, if not free, at least comfortable and able to communicate with one another.

We knew we were heading into war, and although most of the documents and witnesses I had requested were not available, there would be one or two CIA agents present, and Henry was anxious to have at them. The first witness called had seen what he believed to be a person in the back of a truck at about the time that Chuyen had disappeared. I cross-examined him, as Henry was still thumbing through the record of the earlier hearing. Military defense counsel took his testimony apart, inch by inch, to give Henry time to prepare himself. My questions, in part, were as follows:

Q: You are not at all certain, are you, that it was a person on that litter?
A: I am not positive.
Q: Not a bit, and in fact, you have quite a bit of doubt in your mind as to whether or not it was a person or something else, is that correct?
A: I can't . . .
Q: It could have been a big duffle bag, couldn't it?
A: I don't remember.

The hearing droned on, the heat was incredible, the tension

palpable. Finally, it was time to call the CIA agent, whose name still, as of the date of this writing, may not be disclosed, and who is identified throughout the record merely as WITNESS. The investigating officer warned us that the witness would testify but that he "shall confine his testimony to the limited area of what transpired in contacts with defendants concerning the Chuyen case." I jumped to my feet to make it clear that we were not going to waive any rights: "I think we will ask a number of questions and he may state his immunity and refuse to answer. . ."

The witness arrived with his statement prepared and requested that he be allowed to "read a chronology" of his contact with Special Forces and his knowledge of the case. His prepared statement was quite lengthy, and portions of it are still classified secret and deleted from the available record. He did not deny that he had met with some of the defendants to discuss Chuyen. He did deny that there was any solid evidence that Chuyen was a double agent, or that Chuyen had done any harm to our intelligence operations, or was in a position to do any harm in any event. He specifically denied that the CIA had ordered Chuyen "terminated with extreme prejudice," and in fact he stated that the CIA does not involve itself with assassinations, and that even if the CIA were involved in killings, the Agency would have had no authority to have either ordered the Green Berets to carry out such a mission, or to have approved the killing.

It was clear that his reality differed from ours. He denied that the CIA had given any instructions for a cover-up, and the more he talked, the clearer it became that in his opinion the CIA functioned largely as an adjunct to the Boy Scouts or the International Red Cross. He and subsequent witnesses gave an outline as to how the case arose. A certain Sergeant Smith had formed the opinion, sometime after June 20, 1969, that the defendants were acting in a cool and unfriendly manner toward him; he had gone to the CIA headquarters in Nha Trang and had asked for sanctuary. The various witnesses and documents showed that immediately thereafter the CIA (for whatever motives) became extremely concerned about the location and welfare of Chuyen and had inquired from 5th Special Forces Group as to his well-being, and the 5th Special Forces had responded that Chuyen had been sent on a mission. General Abrams was then advised and had called Colonel Rheault in to speak with him.

Part of what the CIA witness said, however, coordinated precisely with what our testimony would have been, had we gone to trial. He stated that one of the defendants asked him, "Don't you have an island or an area where we could geographically seal this guy up for the duration of the war so he won't talk?" After lunch, we began with requesting papers and documents he had referred to.

The investigating officer summarily denied our requests, but I was struck by one phrase made by the witness that opened the door to the issue of terminations: "He has brought up the issue under oath that we don't assassinate; the CIA doesn't do it. Since he has decided to take that course under oath, this becomes relevant and material. . . . I most urgently renew my earlier request that we get a list of all assassinations, or unilateral or bilateral or multilateral terminations with extreme prejudice."

Henry's cross-examination was thorough, lengthy, and exhaustive. He was doing what he does best and doing it with gusto. Among other things, Henry pursued the statement that I had already suggested, and the witness's testimony is interesting primarily because of its evasiveness.

Q: This was discussed as one of the alternatives, a life being sacrificed, is that correct?
A: I don't know about that.
. . .   . . .
Q: Well, you tell us.
A: I am a voluntary witness.
Q: Well, Mr. ———, I assume we all have the same interest in this case. All we are interested in is having the truth of what took place. Whether a person is brought here voluntarily or involuntarily, all I want to know is what happened. Don't you think that is a reasonable request?

A: What is your question again?

Henry's cross-examination went on for hours. Mine was shorter, and I here set forth those parts of my cross-examination that were crucial to the case.

Q: You initiallly received the cable that said that a unilateral net had been compromised, is that right, sir?

A: Yes.

Q: So, would it be a fair statement to say that a compromise of a net can cost lives of Americans and friendly Vietnamese?

A: (Witness nodded his head in the affirmative.)

Q: And this Chuyen, this Vietnamese in question, was the man, according to the cable, who was responsible for that, is that correct, sir?

A: Yes.

. . .

Q: So, when these nets are blown, would it be safe to say it is bad, not only from the standpoint of the GIs or the allies who are killed, but also bad from the standpoint of international relations with the government of Vietnam?

A: It is possible. It depends on how fast it is blown.

. . .

Q: Sir, we appreciate your having come here voluntarily, and as Mr. Rothblatt indicated, your testimony this morning indicated that you very thoroughly prepared yourself and we thank you for that. And, I wonder, sir, if you might consent or consider voluntarily talking to us again when we can do it with a polygraph? Would you do that?

A: I will have to get permission from headquarters.

Marty Linsky had fun with the CIA agent's claim that one of the reasons the CIA agent would not have ordered the killing was that, without doubt, the Vietnamese already knew about B-57. Marty asked the agent if he knew what the nature of B-57's unilateral operations were:

A: This is the first I have ever heard of it.

Q: How can you be so sure then? I mean, if you are a CIA for the United States and you don't know about it, what makes you think the Vietnamese would know about it?

We went from CIA agent to CID agent, from Central Intelligence to Criminal Investigation, across issues regarding availability of witnesses, chain of command, knowledge and lack of knowledge. The government held fast to their position that this was a garden variety conspiracy to commit murder case, that the CID had scrupulously protected the rights of the individuals when taking statements, that Chuyen was a fine citizen, and that our questions were petty and irrelevant.

Still, we chipped away.

In any military trial, the gravest possible error is "command influence." After all, the "separation of powers" doctrine does not exist in the military. The investigating officer is appointed by a command that 1) will decide whether or not to prosecute, and 2) will appoint the officers who sit on the court-martial. So any attempt by the command to influence a military judicial decision will not only result in a reversal of any conviction but will prevent the case from ever being retried. The spectre of command influence flickered light and dark, and the case chugged along through dry throats and incredible heat, moments of anger and exhaustion, and there were moments of interest.

Steve Shaw attempted to get the catalog of CIA weapons, and I joined in his request by making the following statement: "Sir, in reference to this catalog, I would like to see it too, because I am interested in some of the weapons that the CIA has. And I think since they do not assassinate, they don't participate in killing people, I would like to see some of these fancy weapons they have and I think it might tell us a good deal about the nature of their operations."

We got as much information as we could, then it was time for closing arguments. I spoke first:

> . . . It is a simple case, . . . these men are being left, as Mr. Roth-
> blatt said in his questioning, "holding the bag." . . . The govern-
> ment can do one of two things. It can maintains its operations in
> Vietnam, it can maintain its CIA, it can maintain its operations

in Cambodia, or it can try our clients. That is the choice. The government is not going to get it both ways. My men do not have to waive their right to public trial. . . . The government has got a choice, and it is a clear choice.

. . . One of the practical reasons why this case cannot go to trial is the fact that the American people aren't going to put up with it. Colonel Rheault is a hero to the American people like Boucher was, but Boucher was captured by the North Koreans. Colonel Rheault has been captured by the Americans. . . . Do you think the American people are going to put up with this? . . . Everybody in this room knows there is not a military court in the world that would convict one of these men. Every man in this room knows to go to court on this would be a mere exercise of pure bureaucratic inertia. What we need is a little guts and to say, "Okay, the evidence has been examined thoroughly. It is a wonderful job. That is it, the charges are dismissed, the men are released." . . . It is what justice demands; it is what the practical function of the law demands; it is what our operation in Vietnam demands; it is what our situation back home demands. There is no possible excuse for continuing this matter any longer. . . .

We have gone through the whole thing, and the government hasn't come up with a case. The government doesn't have any kind of a corpus. They certainly have no admissible statements. They didn't bring in one witness that told the truth. They didn't bring in one witness that would be believed by any military court. The government has nothing. The government cannot possibly consider taking this case to trial. And, for that reason, let's finish it now.

Several of my co-counsel merely seconded my remarks rather than making their own arguments. Steve Shaw said, "I am still very curious as to the whereabouts of Colonel ———. He is a material witness here and no one seems to even know of his whereabouts. I know not why governmental immunity should keep us from this material. . . . If there are any other materials that you are considering, we do have a right to all of those materials."

Steve had been a good, hard-working co-counsel throughout the case. By demeanor and appearance he was somewhat of a conservative, understated person, his competence always apparent. I enjoyed working with him.

Marty Linsky then spoke: "There was a word mentioned earlier today. The word was grant of immunity. It is a dirty word. I don't like to see that word used in regard to these eight accused. . . . Now, what has been proved is nothing. There is no proof that anybody is dead. If there is no proof that anybody is dead, then there is certainly no proof of a murder. There is no proof of a conspiracy. There is talk of a lot of meetings between a lot of people, but conspiracy implies an agreement and there has been no proof of any agreement."

Then came time for Henry to speak.

Henry gave the investigative officer (and whoever might eventually read the record) a lengthy and thorough lecture on constitutional process and on the law. He addressed himself to mens rea (evil motive), and he began to zero in on the CIA, stating that the CIA was attempting to cover its own errors. He characterized the CIA as taking the position that "we don't want to give you the facts and we don't want to be subjected to the elementary processes of truth finding."

Henry concluded by saying: "Let's say to every soldier fighting this war, 'We will respect your rights; we will respect those basic principles.' Tell the American people that we love our men; we will give them due process rights and not kangaroo court rights, and let the men honestly devote themselves to duty and do what their consciences and their obligations to their country compel them to do. Say to them, 'We will not stand behind the deception, the cover-up by an agency that invokes the privilege,' and promptly dismiss the charges and return these men to honorable duty."

The hearing had lasted four days, July 31 and August 2, and August 20 and 21. Henry had become a hero with the media, at the defendants' holding barracks, and in the officers' club. He would now return to New York to keep the defense pressure on from there.

Bill Hart, Marty Linsky, and I met with Henry at the Cara-

velle Hotel in Saigon to draft a motion directly to President
Nixon, as commander in chief. It struck us as being good strategy to bring the political pressures to the very top. We drew up,
signed, and filed our application. Our motion was for dismissal,
or in the alternative a request for a new Article 32 investigation.
One of Henry's correspondent friends did the typing.

Our document alleged that "the proceedings had been
tainted by command influence of Gen. Creighton Abrams." We
further stated that the Article 32 investigating officer "was and
still is a member of the staff of . . . General Abrams," and we
stated that General Mabry "has acted as policeman, prosecutor
and now purports to act as an impartial convening authority.
He personally ordered the confinement of the accused . . . was
anxious to see the accused convicted because of his subordinate
relationship to Gen. Creighton Abrams . . . commanding general, United States Army Vietnam." We further alleged that the
"Article 32 investigation . . . was totally inadequate . . . and
that the CIA witness repeatedly declined to answer most of the
questions submitted to him by counsel." Our motion was
lengthy, but the central point was that a hearing ordered by
anybody other than by the President of the United States "would
be a nullity because of the command influence exercised by
Gen. Creighton Abrams."

We prayed that our motion be granted without delay, and
that General Abrams be present and subject to examination.
Our intention in drawing up the motion to the President of the
United States, and in letting the press know what we were
doing, was to force Nixon himself to make the decision. We were
certain that there was no legal way he could rule against us, and
we wanted to put political pressure on him.

Henry was ready to leave, but there were problems to be
solved first. We had discovered that our mail was being tampered with. Letters from Henry to me had been opened and
obviously read before I had received them. One of the reporters
made his wire facility available to us so I could send coded messages back to the States. The elaborate code we worked out was

never used. It is mentioned here only to demonstrate our fear of
government interference with our defense—and the willingness
of the press to help us in any way they could.

Rothblatt had chosen "Leaf" for his name, so we based the
other names around it. I believe Edward Bennet Williams (who
would be entering his appearance for Rheault) was "Orchid,"
F. Lee Bailey (for Marasco) was "Lily," and I was "Goldenrod"
—the Nebraska state flower. We had code names for General
Abrams, President Nixon, and almost everybody else who was
in any manner involved in the case or its decision-making
process; we also had code phrases that reflected certain activities. Henry left, taking with him gifts and messages for the
wives.

It was an exhilarating time and place to be a young lawyer.
Once, near curfew time, I had walked through the Saigon side
streets with Henry, looking for the apartment of a correspondent
and his lovely Chinese girl friend. They served us a dinner that
was, by our standards, spectacular. We drank wine and listened
to the stereo, while gunfire roared in the street below.

We now had to wait for the Article 32 investigating officer
to turn the typed transcription of testimony and proceedings
over to General Mabry, along with his recommendation. Of
course, there would be a pretrial advice, written by Colonel
Persons or his staff, suggesting that the case be referred to trial,
or not. All we could do was wait, and during the waiting period,
we lawyers got back to our other cases. Whatever our other
tasks, Marty, Bill, and I tried to get back to Long Binh as often
as possible to see the men. A very real friendship developed
among all the lawyers and the defendants. As a technical matter, the men were restricted and had no right to booze. Of
course, I brought over bottles of Scotch, bourbon, and gin the
first chance I got. The men by now were receiving gifts, cards,
and letters from all over the United States and Europe. Rheault,
who had at first seemed so Spartan as to be inaccessible, showed
me his subtle, wry wit—I had been prepared for his precise and
piercing intellect; it was his genuine warmth that had surprised

me. But his informality had its limitations. One Saturday night somebody brought a pornographic film and a projector over to the barracks. A few of us thought it would at least break the monotony to have a few drinks and enjoy the show. Rheault would not watch the film, but he thought it might be good for his men's morale, so he stood at the door as guard, while we drank and watched and laughed.

David Crew was deeply religious and spent at least an hour a day reading his Bible. He was not morbid or fanatical in any sense of the word. It was his honest belief that this was a real opportunity for a Christian to test and examine his faith. He spoke often of his wife and children. Like Rheault, he was genuinely concerned with the spirit and morale of the other men. Lee Brumley, Budge Williams, Eddie Boyle, and Bob Marasco were very tough men who saw the murder charge as another wartime problem. Boyle was a Bronx Irishman who never seriously doubted the outcome of the case. Williams and Marasco had chilling stories of their adventures in the world of spies and snake eaters. In addition to the pressure of standing trial for murder in Vietnam, Bob Marasco had to face the fact that his marriage was unraveling. Lee Brumley was the quietest of the defendants. When he and I spent time alone, he devoted it to discussing his wife Karen and their small daughter. He was less a swashbuckler than Williams or Marasco but a very good and very tough officer in his own right.

Emotionally, it was a strange time for defense counsel. We had devoted a year to the rapid solution of unrelated problems. We had prided ourselves on being too professional to become personal friends with our clients. Now, suddenly, there was a new kind of pressure—jumping from building to building holding a live baby is one thing, but when that baby is *your own* . . .

I measured my days in terms of how often I could meet with Brumley and the other men. Daily I brainstormed with Linsky and Hart and wrote to Rothblatt. A drink, some conversation, some planning and plotting—the rapport and trust between defense counsel and accused grew to such a point that the young red-haired MP—who had been assigned to the barracks as a "screw"—became an anxious and willing participant in our dreams of victory and freedom.

In the meantime, we were in a frantic search of the law, to find out exactly how far we could go in cross-examining the CIA. We found a July 8, 1969 case from the United States Court of Appeals for the Fifth Circuit. That case, *Casey et al.* v *United States of America*, was decided before a three-judge panel including Circuit Judge Carswell, whom Nixon had unsuccessfully nominated for the Supreme Court.

The defendants in that case had been charged with a two count indictment of conspiring against the Republic of Haiti. According to the decision, "on cross-examination of government witnesses counsel for the defendant twice asked questions that implied that the United States gave . . . support to the defendants' enterprise." In that case the prosecutor had moved that the defendants should not be allowed to ask questions implying that the CIA had engaged in activities supporting the expedition *without first proferring evidence that there was a factual basis for the questions.* That case didn't bother us one bit. We had no intention of asking any questions to which we ourselves did not know the answer. And we had plenty. One of our clients, for instance, could testify as to how and where Che Gueverra had died, and at whose hands.

There had been a Green Beret captain assigned to B-57 who had been charged earlier with the murder of Inchian Hai Lam, a Cambodian who had been working for the Green Berets. The captain, who had been an acquaintance of Budge Williams, had admitted that in the early morning hours of November 24, 1967, he was in a car on a road outside of Saigon, holding a .38 caliber revolver, questioning the Cambodian. According to accounts of that trial, that captain's defense counsel had agreed to the trial being closed at whatever parts were classified as secret. The captain was convicted and sentenced to life imprisonment. On appeal, his attorneys had alleged that he was "suddenly thrust into the world of spies and double agents without the benefit of special training," and that the captain had been "living as a civilian with the civilian population in a capital of a foreign nation . . . under the direct control of a civilian agency of the U.S. government."

The captain in question and his defense counsel had doubtless believed that the honorable and patriotic thing to do was to allow the government to decide what parts of the trial would be public and what parts would be held in secrecy. Their reward was a conviction and a life sentence for a captain, who always maintained that he did not fire the shot that killed Lam. We had no intention of being so accommodating in our defense of the Green Berets.

Any defense counsel who willingly allows any part of any trial to be closed for national security reasons is making a serious mistake. If the government does not want an open trial, the obvious remedy is to dismiss charges. After all, the Sixth Amendment to the Constitution of the United States begins with the words "In all criminal prosecutions, the accused shall enjoy the right to a speedy and public trial. . . ."

The amendment, now less famous and controversial than the First, Fourth, Fifth, and Fourteenth, is a favorite of defense lawyers. It goes on to promise the accused the right "to have compulsory process for obtaining witnesses in his favor, and to have the Assistance of Counsel for his defense."

On August 28, 1969, Secretary of the Army Stanley Resor held a press conference at Tan Son Nhut Airport, Saigon. During that statement, he told the press, "I am sure you would like to have me say a word about the Special Forces case. . . . I appreciate the great public interest which has arisen concerning the case, however, . . . I don't think that it would be appropriate for me to release any further information. . . . I am satisfied that the case is being properly handled by all concerned."

During the question period, he admitted that he had been in communication with General Abrams and further admitted that the men had been under arrest for several days before the

Pentagon knew of the case. He stood up bravely under questioning that bordered on the sarcastic:

Q: Has there been any change in the orders to army commanders that their mission is the pursuit and destruction of enemy forces?

A: Only what Mr. Laird has indicated.

The secretary (whose signature, ironically, appears on my Bronze Star citation) was playing hide and seek. He did send a memorandum to Defense Secretary Laird, who, in turn, sent his own lengthy memorandum to Nixon. Laird's document, which is almost identical to the one Resor sent him, concludes with this language:

> My inquiries disclose that the case has been properly handled by the authorities in Vietnam, and the rights of the accused will be fully protected during trial and appellate review of the proceedings. Under the new Military Justice Act, motions for change of venue, dismissal of the charges, and any other relief should be directed to the military judge assigned to hear the case.
>
> Recommendations: I recommend that no action be taken at this time to preclude trial or otherwise alter the disposition of this case.

VIII

As the men waited in their restriction barracks, Colonel Rheault had emphatically taken command. At the outset, he set up a program for physical training. Rheault, Brumley, and others who enjoyed running over five miles each morning, created a problem for the MPs who were supposed to accompany the prisoners wherever they went. It soon became obvious to the guards that if they did so, they would be the best-conditioned MPs in Vietnam. Finally, it came time to talk. One MP suggested to Rheault and Brumley that they were free to run wherever they wanted to run, that they could run without escort, and that they would be free to do their PT as they wished, if they would give their words of honor not to escape. Rheault and Brumley immediately promised not to escape, and from that time on they could, at any time they wanted, have run out the front gate of Long Binh to wherever they wanted to go.

In addition to PT, Rheault ordered a daily officer's call at 5:00. There were drinks and fellowship, and Marty Linsky, Bill Hart, and I made it a point to be at Long Binh by 5:00 whenever possible. Letters of support and packages continued to arrive from Americans and Europeans who had heard or read of the case, and the men developed their own humor. One was a lengthy discussion of their potential incarceration: Brumley said that he would want to be assigned to the car wash at Fort Leavenworth, and that whenever he had to wash a car belonging to a "leg," he would be sure and scratch the finish. Whenever I would make a particularly outrageous remark, Lee would raise an eyebrow at Budge, and they would say in unison, "Well, back to the tunnel." There were constant joking conversations of means of escape should our legal efforts fail.

Yet, the idea of a rescue mission was not entirely facetious. A package was smuggled into Budge Williams, containing a false passport, a 9mm pistol, and some hand grenades. In this particular war, the rules of patriotism and good soldiering were difficult to define, and we were fully aware of a contingent of American soldiers who would rather bring down fire power on Long Binh than allow these men to go to trial.

Some of the war's truly legendary characters began to drop in to see what they could do. Larkin W. (Rocky) Nesom, a dark, handsome soldier of fortune type, who had been a master sergeant under Rheault and was now flying one of the clandestine air routes, had suggested to Bob that in the event of a bad decision, Nesom and his men would stop by in a Dornier, a German light aircraft especially good for short takeoffs and landings, and rescue Rheault and the men. Nesom liked to entertain Rheault by quoting Kipling, and in addition to his discussions of a rescue mission, he had perhaps a more serious threat to the prosecution: he would use his leave time to round up Special

Forces alumni and gather evidence to educate the public as to the manner in which the war was actually being fought.

This latter suggestion was tempting in its way. The CIA agent had stated under oath that the CIA does not order assassinations. Although our primary defense was simply that the government had no case, it struck us that this would be an excellent route for rebuttal evidence. If we were forced to trial, and if the CIA continued to lie, we would be able to bring in rebuttal witnesses to show the nature and depth of the lie. We would make the army regret having ever brought the matter to trial.

Rheault accepted the information that Nesom and others had brought to him with a certain amount of reluctance. He was, after all, a military man, and he was as worried over the harm the army appeared to be intent upon inflicting upon itself as he was concerned about the safety of himself and his men.

I was never particularly concerned about the rescue mission because I honestly did not believe there was any way the army would ever bring the case to trial, or, if they did, I did not see how we could lose. Still, the idea of a planned armed rescue from a trial was not a new concept in the lore of my own family. Many years ago my grandfather, John Stevens, had defended one of his brothers, Ott Stevens (an elected city marshal) in a first degree murder trial. The case had arisen from his attempt to arrest the leader of a group staging a planned disorder on the frontier streets of Arapahoe, Nebraska. John Stevens was successful in his defense which was not surprising since he was an excellent lawyer and, according to Tunnard Stevens (who is old enough to at least remember the stories), the back of the courtroom was filled with Stevens men with ill-concealed pocket guns. The Stevens men were there to provide moral support to the judge, a longtime family friend, and to discourage friends of the "victim" from staging a courtroom takeover. The Stevens men also undoubtedly provided moral support for what appeared to be a somewhat intimidated and shaky jury.

Despite Rheault's constant concern with morale, the men grew increasingly bitter. While they were confined, it was made public that an airborne colonel from the Vietnamese Army had shot and killed two American MPs in a Saigon bar. Both were wounded when he finished them off on the floor. The American government never pushed for the Vietnamese to prosecute the colonel and no legal action was taken against the Vietnamese officer. Budge liked to discuss the fact that although the navy had sent two ships from Japan to Nha Trang Bay to search for Chuyen's body, no such naval missions had been used to attempt to rescue or find American soldiers whose helicopters had crashed in the bay.

Bob Rheault was commanding a small but difficult group of men, all strong individualists. He was not particularly happy about Williams's possession of weapons and false passports and would have been enraged if he had heard that Williams had been slipping out of the barracks some evenings to parties in Long Binh and even Saigon! Budge Williams was, after all, a "good old boy," and he was going to have his fun, as best he could under the circumstances.

Perhaps the most important visitor we had in the barracks in those days was Col. Charles M. "Bill" Simpson III, who was commander of the 1st Special Forces Group in Okinawa, Rheault's old command. When I first met him, he and Rheault were visiting as old friends do, about the days when they were assigned to occupation forces in Europe right after World War II —Simpson in Austria, Rheault first with the constabulary on the Czechoslovakian border, later on the Russian-German border. Rheault introduced me to Simpson as "the sloppiest soldier and the best lawyer in Vietnam." I later learned that they were "career twins" in the sense that they had finished West Point together in 1946, had gone to Fort Benning Infantry School together, and then, at different times, had gone to Airborne School, attended the Command and General Staff College, and had entered into the Special Forces.

Apparently, when they were both assigned to the West Point faculty, they lived across the street from one another, and they and their families had become fast friends.

Bob Rheault's wife, Nan, had asked Simpson to help when she learned of Bob's incarceration, and Simpson had rushed to Vietnam to see what he could do. He arrived on August 4, knew that his old friend was in trouble, but had no facts. When Simpson and his sergeant major arrived, the Special Forces delegation that met his plane in Saigon told him that they had located Rheault. They took Simpson to the trailer where Rheault was being held in confinement.

They talked for several hours, and Simpson agreed to return the next day to spend the night with Rheault. Colonel Simpson then flew north to visit his temporary duty troops to touch base with his men. He sent word back to the provost marshal that he would return on August 6 and would spend the night with Rheault. But on August 6, when Simpson landed in Saigon, he learned that the army had gone public the previous day. Perhaps the command had thought that he would break the news, though if that was what they thought, they had badly misjudged him. Simpson was escorted to the provost marshal that night, and after lengthy argument, he was finally allowed to go to Rheault's trailer. But Simpson was ordered to sleep in the adjoining trailer. Because he had brought steaks and Scotch with him, he and Bob Rheault ate, drank, and talked until midnight.

The next day Simpson wrote to Abrams's office, asking for an interview. He did get to see Abrams's deputy for two hours. Simpson and his command sergeant major decided to hide out in a safe house that afternoon, and that evening they tried to get aboard a midnight plane to Okinawa. After they had belted up, two military police arrested them, took them off the plane without explanation, and put them in a trailer for the night. The next morning they were escorted to the next plane for Okinawa.

Simpson had seen enough to know that his close friend was in danger, and he decided that he would do what he could for Bob Rheault, no matter what the results to Simpson's own career. He took his two teenage daughters back to the United States on August 10 and headed for Washington, D.C. From then until the end of the lawsuit, he would be walking the halls of the Pentagon, buttonholing acquaintances, trying to bring influence to bear on Rheault's behalf.

Defense counsel saw Simpson as a mysterious but powerful ally. From him we learned what was being said at the Pentagon, what the rumors were, and where to apply the pressure. It did not strike Simpson at all remarkable that he was ready to sacrifice his own career to help a friend. That was the kind of loyalty that Bob Rheault instinctively gave, and received in return.

Simpson reported back to us that the president had wanted to dismiss the case, but that Abrams had told Nixon to keep his nose out of Abrams's business if Nixon wanted a nice quiet withdrawal from Vietnam. Simpson had been in contact with his old friend Alexander Haig, and it was Simpson's opinion that Haig, Nixon, and Kissinger all wanted the case dismissed, but that Nixon had bowed to Abrams's pressures. And Simpson reported back on Rheault's replacement as commander of the Green Berets.

Rheault was replaced by a Colonel Lemberes, who had immediately donned the green beret, only to be advised by his sergeant major that he could not wear the hat since he was not airborne. Lemberes, then, rather than go through the training program and have five jumps from an airplane, went down to Don Ba Thin, a small Vietnamese training camp south of Nha Trang, took three jumps from a helicopter, broke his leg on the third jump, and awarded himself jump wings. His entire performance, and the way he was regarded by his men, had enraged Westmoreland, who had in turn told Abrams that there should be a real airborne officer commanding the 5th Special Forces Group. One of Simpson's sources reported that Simpson himself had been recommended to take the job as commander of the group, and Abrams, aware of Simpson's work on behalf of Rheault, was reported to have said, "Hell, no, that son of a bitch stuck his nose in my business—I'll see to it that he never commands the 5th Special Forces Group and that he won't make general either." Lemberes was later convicted of fraud in Nevada.

There is one final twist in the Rheault/Simpson/Lemberes relationship. Years after the Green Beret case was disposed of, after Lemberes had been convicted in Federal Court, he apparently attempted to use his military record as a matter to be considered on his behalf in connection with sentencing. Somebody had asked the presentence investigation people to contact Rheault regarding Lemberes's character and military history, and Rheault was pleased to say that even Lemberes's jump wings were fraudulently obtained.

The army still had not ordered the men to trial, and we remained optimistic, certain that the case would be dismissed. Then, one fine day, Colonel Rector called and ordered me to appear in Colonel Persons's office at 9:00 P.M. I doubt that I could ever forget that sequence of events, but if I did, I would be aided by the following transcription of my testimony, given months later, at the Pentagon: "Colonel Rector talked to me and told me not to tell anybody I was going to be at the meeting, and not to discuss the meeting. Well, of course, I first had to tell Colonel Jones I was going to a meeting at nine that evening because I had to get a vehicle." Here was the office of the USARV staff judge advocate again, telling me with whom I could not speak, and about what we could speak.

Months later, at the Pentagon, I had this to say about the meeting where we were advised that the cases were being ordered to trial, and our motions to dismiss were denied: "We were called to Colonel Persons's office and went in at nine o'clock; . . . I then said, 'Sir, there is a brief period of time now. I would like for my client to be able to advise his family that these charges are being referred, prior to their finding out by the media; the media will release it soon. I would like a head start.' He said there was no legal right for my client to do that. I then said to Colonel Persons, 'Sir, I am not talking about legal rights; I am talking about the basic elements of human decency.' "

Colonel Rector was also questioned about that incident, and he remembered it differently from my recollection:

RECTOR: There were sides that some of us felt the case should be tried. On the other hand, there were defense counsel who felt that the case shouldn't be tried. So, therefore, immediately the night that they told that the case was going to trial, I will never forget it, all the counsel sitting in that room, their faces dropped as if you had dropped a bomb right in the middle of them . . . one of the counsel jumped up and was actually disrespectful to the staff judge advocate at that time.

Q: Captain Berry.

RECTOR: Captain Berry. He started shouting and ranting.

X

So now it was go. Henry Rothblatt was cranked up and ready to roll—with the Caravelle document and others. Henry was now co-counsel for Brumley, Crew, and Boyle. Edward Bennett Williams was entering the case on behalf of Rheault, and F. Lee Bailey was entering on behalf of Bob Marasco. Guy B. Scott from Athens, Georgia, entered his appearance for Budge Williams. The army had moved Boyle out of the barracks, and had decided to keep Eddie separate from the other men, and to offer him immunity, and to compel him to testify. Eddie told me, "I have only two words for the army, and they are not 'Merry Christmas.' "

Eddie was past his rotation date, and since he was granted immunity, theoretically he could not be held in Vietnam because there was an army directive that a person could not be held in Vietnam past his normal rotation date for the sole purpose of testifying. But Eddie was being held anyway, and the army began to issue certain Catch-22 memoranda, including the statement that Warrant Officer Boyle's records were flagged, and since they were flagged, no favorable action could be taken. So of course Henry filed a writ of habeas corpus in the Federal Court in San Francisco.

It was time to come out with guns blazing. I met with the press and appeared on network television two nights running.

The army had been issuing their own press releases, and by God the American public was going to hear our side of the story, too. I said, "There are fair trials and there are closed trials, but a trial cannot be both closed and fair." I said, "I predict that our government will have to choose between trying this lawsuit and waging this war."

Colonel Persons maintained a log, parts of which are available and parts of which are not available. Among those unclassified parts, there is a note of September 27, 1969, that ". . . informed . . . that although I am aware of the apparent violations of AR 190-4 on press interviews and of paragraph 42B MCM, on newspaper, radio or television comment by military counsel, I did not intend to remonstrate with them, as any comment would be misconstrued as an effort to intimidate. Example is a report in the letter . . . from California that Captain Berry has been several times on network television, making various allegations about General Abrams's personal involvement in the case."

And the army was facing certain other problems. A number of congressmen, headed by Rodino, began to launch vigorous attacks on the government's handling of the case. Rodino made a powerful speech on the floor of the House:

> Mr. Speaker. One of the weirdest—probably cruelest—trials in the military history of this nation is about to unfold in far-off Vietnam. . . . So great is my indignation—and so deep my dismay—over the handling of the Green Berets that I must speak out. . . . We have an obligation to assure not only our servicemen but also all of our citizens these men will not be deserted by us. . . . Officials in the Pentagon, officials from the CIA and commanders in the field have already violated the code of military justice by leaking to the press their own self-serving and distorted versions of the incident. . . . When they were arrested, the servicemen were placed in five by seven foot cells under maximum security in the Long Binh stockade. They were denied proper ventilation, light and other appropriate facilities. . . . The Pentagon appears to have totally isolated itself from the forces

in the field by a chasm of vast dimension. At a time when our president . . . was in a direct communication with the Sea of Tranquility on the moon, not one official in the Pentagon was concerned with the ocean of ignorance that separated Washington from our fighting men in Vietnam.

A young military justice officer sent a copy of this speech on to his superiors, suggesting it as "light reading." As late as September 23, the prosecution had not understood that we would enlist the nation as our ally. Put another way, the issues were now more political than legal. We planned on winning on both fronts.

Meanwhile, other good questions were arising in Congress.

Curiously, it was only Nebraska's Senator Roman Hruska who thought to ask exactly what was the function of the Green Berets. The answer was fascinating:

U.S. Army Special Forces . . . composed of military personnel who have received training in basic and specialized army skills . . . have extensively cross-trained to provide depth in small unit capabilities . . . multipurpose forces which can . . . address a variety of missions . . . plan and conduct unconventional warfare operations . . . for military, political or economical offices within an area controlled by the enemy and employ local inhabitants and resources . . . guerrilla warfare, escape and evasion and subversion . . . plan . . . that type of internal defense . . . to maintain, restore or establish a climate of order within which responsible governments can function effectively . . . plan and conduct direct action missions which are peculiar to Special Forces due to their organization, training, equipment and psychological preparation . . . highly specialized assignments which are directed against special strategic targets the destruction of which have been determined to be mandatory . . .

Sen. Mendel Rivers, who was chairman of the committee on armed services, wrote to Secretary Laird: "This case is going from bad to worse . . . frankly, the members of the committee on armed services are getting a little bit disturbed by the manner in which the only information made available to us comes

from the newspapers." U.S. Senator Hollings sent the following
telegram to Secretary Laird: "Your handling of the Green Beret
case threatens to compromise our intelligence activities and
gives the Green Berets a black eye." On September 24, Congressman Hanley wrote to Secretary Laird that he felt com-
pelled "to express my great dissatisfaction with the handling of
the arrest of the members of the Fifth Special Forces Group on
charges of murder and conspiracy to commit murder. The
American people are in a state of confusion over this matter.
The confusion which is rapidly changing to indignation and
anger is the responsibility of the Department of the Army . . ."

The American public had become impassioned. I have in
my possession well over a thousand letters that became part of
the official records. One mother sent in the leaflet missal for the
Mass on the Day of Burial, for her son who was killed in action
in Vietnam, January 6, 1969. At the beginning, for the proces-
sion to the church, the priest quotes from Psalm 130: "Out of
the depths I cry to You, Oh, Lord. Lord, hear my voice!" And a
woman from Ohio wrote: "I get a sick feeling all over my body
when I hear and read these things. Please turn these men loose;
don't ruin their lives."

A mother with a son in Vietnam wrote to President Nixon:
"The mothers I have talked to have all agreed the boys in the
field are the ones who need bolstering . . . the court-martial of
the Special Forces men is a disgrace; they are doing nothing but
making scapegoats of them . . . the people are going to revolt."
And President Nixon received this letter dated September 23,
1969: ". . . I have never been so horrified and disturbed over an
incident . . . as that of the situation of . . . the Green Berets. . . . I
feel very strongly that these men have been betrayed by the
United States government . . . our poor son is serving in Vietnam
—a voluntary infantryman. Am I to understand that he is in
jeopardy of being accused of murder . . . he might today be in
the situation of those six men who the army and the CIA are
attempting to set up as scapegoats. If General Abrams had any
part in this set up (as reported in a reliable news dispatch of this

week) then he must be the master Judas Iscariot of the 20th century . . . I am a Republican committee woman . . ."

Many of the letters set forth the history of the writers as Republicans who had managed campaign offices or had been committee workers, or substantial contributors to President Nixon, who wanted to make it clear that they had spent years carrying water to the elephant and thought they had earned the right to a hearing. One such letter, from Albany, New York, dated August 28, told Secretary Laird that "I can think of nothing that will lower the morale greater than imprisonment of American soldiers for doing their duties . . . we cannot afford to lose men of the caliber of these officers. We are already losing 100–200 men killed per week. We are not in a tea party. In a war, we must not tie the hands of our soldiers . . . Special Forces are given a dirty job to do; in intelligence or counterguerrilla warfare, they can't use the same methods we'd expect to use in a civilized nation. Unless these men are released soon, I feel that American morale will suffer."

From Madison, Wisconsin, this letter of September 23 to President Nixon: "First, Mr. President, I would like to relate the wording on the Silver Star citation awarded my son posthumously . . . he was [on] one of the first helicopters to set down in a landing zone northeast of Kontum, and immediately assumed the position to provide security for the incoming helicopters. *As the fourth helicopter touched down, an unknown-sized enemy force subjected the landing zone to intense automatic weapons, fortified small arms and mortar fire from their well-concealed fortified positions. . . .*" The letter went on to say that the VC had clearly known in advance that the helicopter was going to land where it did and when it did—perhaps through information given by Chuyen or one like him. It concluded: "Mr. President, I urge you to intervene in the murder charges against our eight great fighting men and give them what they really deserve: A MEDAL FOR GALLANTRY IN ACTION AGAINST AN ENEMY BY KILLING AN AGENT OF THE SAME AND SAVING COUNTLESS NUMBER OF AMERICAN LIVES. . . .

Mr. President, I further request that you institute an investigation to find out who is responsible for this great injustice to our fighting men and bring them to trial for helping an enemy force in time of war."

A letter of September 29 begins: "I'm an American mother who lost my beloved 23 year old son. He was killed in combat . . . in the province of Kian Phong . . . if you let the Green Beret officers stand trial I will curse you until the day I die . . . if you let this trial continue it is a disgrace to American justice." The letter was signed with the woman's name, and above it, "America's Gold Star Mother." Another letter from a mother who had lost a son in Vietnam said: "What do we mothers who have sons over there, and some of us who have lost our sons, and mothers who have sons yet to go and be trained to kill or be killed have to look forward to? . . . Tell me why the Green Berets have to be charged with murder. You know and I know this was what they were trained to do. . . . I lost my son June 14, 1968 in Vietnam—fighting and doing his duty for what?"

Letters from American Legion chapters and American Legion Auxiliary chapters, with hundreds of signatures. Letters from registered Republicans, who united for the purpose of having their boxes of letters hand-delivered to the president. One stated: "It appears that the CIA has bungled again and this time it has brought trouble to some innocent people . . . possibly a human sacrifice is needed to placate the government of South Vietnam." A very short letter to President Nixon, dated August 22, 1969: "We must back our armed forces if we expect them to back us." From Arlington, Virginia: "As a veteran and widow having two boys in Arlington National Cemetery as a result of the Vietnam War, I am deeply offended that the government they died for is prosecuting the Green Beret officers. The military is fighting for the USA. Which side are you on?"

Finally, the political pressure became too much. Congressman George Bush and many other distinguished members of both Houses were demanding answers. On September 29, a statement was issued ordering the case dismissed because "the

Central Intelligence Agency, though not directly involved in the alleged incident, has determined that in the interest of national security it will not make available any of its personnel as witnesses."

XI

That morning, early, there was a pounding at my door. I had just come back from showering and shaving and was in my shorts. My driver stuck his head in the door: "Hey, Captain— Colonel Jones ordered me to drive you to Long Binh immediately. You are not to stop at the office. Get your gear and let's head out!"

Stunned, I got dressed as quickly as I could, and we drove to the barracks where the Green Berets were being kept. There was a cassette playing "The Ballad of the Green Berets" at top volume. Marasco, Middleton, and Brumley ran out and embraced me—an embrace that was photographed by somebody from the AP and appeared the next morning on my mother's doorstep, front page of the *Omaha World Herald*—my head was spinning. Could it be true? But there was no doubt, it was true. I later saw that same picture on the front page of a San Francisco newspaper and next to it was a picture of a weeping Pham Kim Lien, the wife of the disappeared Thai Khac Chuyen. She was quoted as saying that the soul of her husband would haunt whoever was responsible for his death. It was impossible not to grieve for her, and I do. Yet, she stirred up even more controversy by applying for and receiving a death gratuity. She received approximately sixty-five hundred dollars, and certainly she would need it—but there were citizens who resented her receiving payment.

A woman wrote to Sen. John Tower and to President Nixon to ask why Thai Khac Chuyen's wife, Pham Kim Lien, received money from the government. A memorandum to the chief of staff of the United States Army stated, "The widow was paid a death gratuity under regulations of the Fifth Special Forces

Group which provide for such payments to the survivors of the civilian employees of the unit who have been missing more than sixty days and are officially declared dead. Thai Khac Chuyen was such an employee.'' The buck slip from the White House, with the usual action requests, contained this statement: "He was the double agent the Green Berets were accused of killing.'' Well, well. This did seem to run against the official theory that he was a helpless civilian, uninvolved with the CIA. Was the administration actually admitting that the man was a double agent?

The *Washington Post* quoted some official as saying, "There is no evidence that he was dead.''

Did such a person even exist? Somebody interviewed the officers of the minesweeper *Woodpecker* which had, with two other navy vessels, searched for a body for several months.

The case was over.

XII

But of course the case was not over. The people who had been affected by it would never be the same.

Nan Rheault, a lady of obvious refinement, had lived the good life as the wife of a wealthy professional soldier, who was also a member of the social register. A Vassar graduate and an accomplished artist, she had never let her social activities interfere with her home and her children. Then, suddenly, she had found her husband charged with murder. The same summer, Sen. Edward Kennedy had had his accident near Rheault's home on Martha's Vineyard, and the press had camped on Nan Rheault's doorstep, sometimes as a diversion from covering the Kennedy matter. She found herself under siege. She did receive a call from F. Lee Bailey, who asked if she had been calling his office, and she emphatically stated that she had not.

Bob Rheault's family had engaged a certain Mahoney, who then arranged a meeting with Edward Bennet Williams. In August of 1969, Mahoney, Rheault's brother and Nan Rheault flew to Nantucket to talk to Williams at his palatial home. They met in the garden, and Williams turned to Nan and said, "Of course he's guilty as hell! Most of my clients are. We can only expect a fifty-fifty chance of acquittal." Nan Rheault was devastated. She finally composed herself enough to ask what his charge would be, and Williams stated that he would charge "the same as Mahoney." Later, Williams and Mahoney charged Bob Rheault forty thousand dollars for their few days in Vietnam.

Nan had noticed that her mail had been tampered with. Three of Bob's letters to her arrived obviously opened and resealed with tape. And he had received one of her letters in a similar condition. Nan had spoken with politicans, army people —everyone she knew—to try to help Bob. Yet she refused to criticize the army to the press. Her behavior, as one prosecution document states, "was magnificent."

One day, late in September, she was downtown in Boston— and heard the news that the charges had been dismissed. She was elated and rushed home, cherishing her deliverance. But the newsmen were camped all over her apartment house front steps. There were television camera crews awaiting her, and it was perhaps at that moment she knew that neither her life nor her marriage to Bob Rheault would ever be the same again.

XIII

Of course the international press had an interest in reporting the story. The October 18 issue of the *Saturday Review* carried an article entitled "The Ghostly War of the Green Berets." On September 30, the official Soviet News Agency Tass charged that the United States was setting free known murderers in the Green Beret case. And there were articles in *Le Nouvel Observateur* about *Bagatelles pour un Assassinat*. Budge Williams, of course, was irrepressible and was quoted in the *New York Times* as saying, "I regard all enemies as dangerous . . . when you find one, you kill him. That's what they pay me for, not to worry about his social problems."

Times and *Newsweek* ran cover stories on the case. Art

Buchwald wrote a hilarious column in which he addressed the peculiarity of this prosecution in the context of B-52 bombings, body counts, destruction of villages, etc.

There was handshaking and embracing and promises to keep in touch, and then Linsky, Hart and I headed for Saigon for our own private celebration. We had good steaks at one of the BOQs, but we had no intention of spending the night there with the lifers. We found a hotel on Tu Do Street, a distinguished establishment named The Hotel Lower Rent.

As with many Saigon hotels, it was also a whorehouse. It had a balcony overlooking the streets, and Linsky, Hart and I sat there on the balcony, looking out across the empty streets of Saigon, occasionally yelling down the elevator shaft to the desk clerk, who brought us more cold beer. "Papa-San-more Buzz-wie." It is impossible to describe the sense of desolation one feels, after curfew, looking out over a huge and once-great city. Occasional MP jeeps or comsats (The White Mice) and nothing more in the street. Tracer rounds in the distance, bleeding down the sky, reminiscent of Blake:

> When the stars threw down their spears,
> And water'd heaven with their tears . . .

The men later told me that when they got on their Freedom Bird to fly home, the pilot announced their presence, and they were given an ovation. I have it on very good authority that the captains and those of their wives who met them drank a toast "to Berry" at a small but luxurious bar in San Francisco; and my favorite story is that the men and their wives were walking down the streets of San Francisco, when a woman had asked them, "Are you the Green Barrettes?" The men smiled politely, but the women said, "No, *we* are the Green Barrettes, they are the Green Berets."

David Crew, arriving back in Cedar Rapids, Iowa, called my mother and told her that he believed the Lord had sent me to deliver him.

And there were loose ends.

Most of the defendants declined or refused to talk about the case after it was over. Marasco, who had been described as the "trigger man," talked willingly to the press; then, suddenly, he was injured and almost killed in a freak automobile accident. Later, he appeared on several nights with Dick Cavett, discussing his experiences. Bob always wondered if the CIA was in some way responsible for the accident.

After I had returned to the World, a few weeks after the Berets, I went to New York to see Rothblatt, and Henry told me he was going to "recruit me like a star" for his law firm, where I later worked for a year before returning to the Midwest. He sent me off on a vacation to his San Juan, Puerto Rico, condominium, at his expense. Before I left, we sent flowers to the hospitalized Marasco with a nice card signed "Henry Rothblatt, F. Lee Bailey and Steve Berry." Heavy company for a young trial lawyer.

While I was in San Francisco, Henry would call, sometimes just to visit, but occasionally for information for a novel that he and Robin Moore were writing, which was eventually entitled *Court-Martial* and published by Doubleday. I gave some technical advice and was featured as one of the heroes in the book. Henry Rothblatt himself appeared as Hank, the civilian attorney who went to Vietnam to defend some Green Beret officers in a murder case. I was his military counsel, Capt. Steven Brace. I particularly liked the following scene from the novel:

> A big voice boomed from the door. "I'd sure as hell know."
> Steve Brace appeared with his two Nungs, Swedish Ks with silencers and flash suppressors leveled. . . .

There was some bitterness both from the prosecution and the defense, and a Green Beret Captain Sheffield had asked to be removed from the JAG Corps and transferred back to infantry because he felt that his sense of honor and decency had been offended by the behavior and tactics of the prosecution. Sheffield was an excellent officer and lawyer, and I sympathized with his position, but I was prepared to be generous in victory. At the Pentagon hearing which had been scheduled to investigate Sheffield's allegations of prosecutorial misbehavior, I testified as follows. "Would I personally make allegations or charges against Colonel Persons or Colonel Rector? The answer is No. We have a very honorable corps, made up of excellent attorneys; but, like all lawyers, we like to fight."

Newsweek, in its August 25, 1969 cover story on the still-pending case, had included a sidebar about Rheault: "Will He Ever Get His Star?" the title asked. The article—citing Rheault's graduate studies at George Washington University, as well as the intense loyalty he inspired in men who knew him—concluded on an optimistic note. But Colonel Persons and Colonel Rector became General Persons and General Rector, and Bob Rheault and Bill Simpson retired as colonels. After B-57 closed down, the VC/NVA were able to build up their operations at bases in Cambodia with no risk of observation. The VC/NVA used those base areas as part of their final offensive drive in 1975 which destroyed the South Vietnamese Army in weeks. We lost the war.

When Margaret and I were married in September 1972, David Crew came to be an usher; Henry Rothblatt sent a telegram expressing his regrets (he was tied up in the Watergate case) and a beautiful ginger jar from Tiffany's. Marty Linsky is now a federal administrative law judge, and Bill Hart has a private practice in Jerome, Idaho. Once, after successfully defending a Vietnam amputee in a three-week-long heroin case, I met with Eddie Boyle in Baltimore. I received a few good letters from Budge Williams. Lee Brumley and I exchange Christmas cards each year. Lee has sent me some very nice gifts, my favorite of which is a command portrait of himself, inscribed simply: "To Steve Berry, Defender of the Forces." Bob Rheault had earlier given me a command photograph, "To Steve Berry, eloquent and dedicated defender of the Green Berets."

After my DEROS, I returned twice to Vietnam for periods of three weeks each, to represent GIs who had requested me. I was present at Di An when the Big Red One struck their colors and headed home. I went back to the Plantation during those return visits, to see people and places I thought I had lost forever. Crew and Brumley went on to have successful careers in the army, and both rose to the rank of colonel. Budge Williams now owns and operates several successful liquor stores in Athens, Georgia, and in 1972 was the last Special Forces man to haul down the colors at Nha Trang.

Bob Rheault went to work for Outward Bound, stayed there for a number of years, and concluded that the Outward Bound concept would work for Vietnam veterans, especially those with post-traumatic stress disorders. He has dedicated his time and energy to providing group therapy for those post-traumatic veterans whom he is able to take from veteran hospitals for six-day courses. Bob leads his "patients" through a course of camping, hiking, rope climbing, and living in the outdoors, as an adjunct to group therapy. After twenty-six years in the army and thirteen years in Outward Bound, Bob Rheault is working as a volunteer, without pay or funds, making enthusiastic presentations to medical groups, trying to do what he can for Vietnam veterans.

As for the case: perhaps the final commentary was best expressed by the editorial cartoons of the time. I here reproduce the best of those available to me:

They Can Wear Their Berets With Pride

By permission of Eddie Germano, Brockton Daily Enterprise

"YOU'RE EXONERATED!"

By permission of Dobbins and the Boston Herald

Backswing

By permission of Bill Mauldin and Wil-Jo Associates, Inc.

PART FOUR

TWILIGHT ON THE MOON

. . . something inside my head
Flaps like a worn-out blind. . . .
There is no twilight on the moon, no mist or rain,
No hail or snow, no life. Here in this house

Dried ferns keep falling to the floor . . .

—Weldon Kees, "Round"

I THINK OF ALL MY PLEADINGS AND MY JUDGMENTS; of myself and the men I represented. I think of our journey, and of our return, and I try to bring some form and shape to my own ideas of where we had been and what we had done. We came home, much as Gulliver came home, benumbed and awry. He had tried to understand where he had been and what he had done—he had tried to know what had happened to him. Coming home, he found himself seeking understanding from others. Perhaps it was that final denial—his failure to be understood at all—that led to his madness and his rage.

Although his wife and family received him "with great surprise and joy," Mr. Lemuel Gulliver had to "freely confess the sight of them filled me only with hatred, disgust and contempt." During his first year home, he "could not endure my wife or children in my presence . . . much less could I suffer them to eat in the same room." And, Mr. Gulliver tells us, five years after his return, ". . . they dare not presume to touch my bread, or drink out of the same cup, neither was I ever able to let one of them take me by the hand."

The first time in civilian life I represented a Vietnam veteran charged with murder, I found myself looking for the symptoms of post-traumatic stress disorders. Had this one, too, been castrated of his hope glands? In any case, none of us will ever regain our innocent certainty in happy endings.

But some of our memories are darkly lyrical. The ancient Aztecs had made their idols perfect by mixing human blood into materials. That was the only way to put together a good lawsuit in Vietnam: a setting forth of one's selfhood, perhaps in ways that we would never again have the opportunity to do.

In my dreams, sometimes, that year became a kind of light show—the mystic hills of the aboriginal Vietnamese, the strong coloring of the Chinese influence, the fading pastels of the Japanese and French, and the prism of the Americans—perhaps our judicial system being a small light in that band of color—strange, perplexing coincidences.

One of the units I served had a "gone but not forgotten" board: men who went home left a name tag from their jungle fatigues, to be stapled to the board. Then, somebody decided it would be a good idea to include the name tags of people who had died. The board, which had been part of the going-away beerblast, achieved eerie solemnity. It became important, somehow, that one's name be preserved.

When I first learned of the Vietnamese custom of giving children secret names to fool the evil spirits, I thought of the white stone in the Book of Revelation: the one with my new name unknown to all but me.

There are concrete things that stay with me. I once illegally gave a kitchen girl (Ti Ti) some PX candy and soaps for her birthday. She seemed surprised that I wanted nothing in return, and later, whenever she saw me, she would giggle and chant, "Captain Berry, candy and soaps—Captain Berry, candy and soaps . . ."

Secret names. Something from the Book of the Dead: *Iren:* —my name—must survive me, or I will cease to exist . . . my judgment will take place in the Judgment Hall of Osiris, the scale weighing my heart against the feather, and I will be consigned to either the Eater of the Dead at which point my subscription will be cancelled—or I will enter into the domain of Osiris, the Big PX.

And I would walk the rear perimeters when I drew Officer of the Day and be challenged by the GI with a loaded rifle. Beyond the rear perimeter, darkness; and I would go back to the bunker and log in my tour. Sometimes I would think of my great-grandfather, John Stevens, who left his home in Virginia and fought for the Iowa infantry during the American Civil War. I would sleep in the dark, heavy room with the overhead fan moving slowly, and dream of the Montagnards with their animistic practices, of the Bahnar who filed their teeth and wore loincloths; of the Rhade, with their sorcerers and their sacrifices of fowl. Courtrooms in homes and courtrooms in buildings that could have been homes or whorehouses, courtrooms in tents, courtrooms under thatched roofs. Dreaming—patching things together, getting ready for the trip home—dreaming of that weary land. It was a weary land. The sacred Mekong had come twenty-five hundred miles from its source in Tibet, and here we flew over scorched cathedral palms, and from a helicopter you could see the craters where the mortar shells and rockets had made the nights to shudder; year after year, a land weary with whispers and rumors, blending into the scents of a jaded weariness. The old coffin maker in his hammock outside a small village composed of nothing but straw; and water buffalo and hooches and men and women and children.

Vietnam came back to me at strange times and in strange ways. Once I was invited to a party in the San Francisco area. Everybody there had been a Vietnam law captain. Beer, snacks, and good conversation. I left the party and forgot about it. But when Alex Shipley left that party, he went home, wrote out a memorandum about Donald Segretti approaching him and some others, offering employment. Shipley, who later became associated with the office of the attorney general in Tennessee, turned Segretti in. By then, I was back in Nebraska, practicing law. Two FBI agents called on me and advised me that I had been identified under oath as a person to whom such employment was offered. And somebody from Senator Kennedy's subcommittee called me on the telephone to ask me about it. But if I was offered any such job, I was unaware of it at the time. Segretti was eventually convicted for his part in Nixon's "dirty tricks" department and was later portrayed in the film, *All the President's Men.* He was disbarred, but got his license back the same year Shipley died while jogging.

Once, two lurps (men assigned to long-range reconnaissance patrols) came to me and told me they had been offered nonjudicial punishment, but they did not want to accept it because they were afraid they might be brought out of the heart of the fighting, and if they were, they were certain that the cherries (new to the field) would die. Could I please talk to their commanding officer about whatever the trouble was? They quite literally disappeared into the distance. One of them died two days later, "shock from loss of blood" somewhere in the jungle, the legal cloud still hanging over his head. His eyes still burn into me, as they did a dozen years and many thousands of miles ago. I could have done more. And although my military service was one of ease and comfort, still, I know that since my return, I have sometimes behaved badly indeed—as though I were, also, entitled to wear those honorable badges of psychic scars.

And yet, I have still been unable to answer those who ask me to define or describe the law as it was in Vietnam in those days. I knew of a pilot who had flown missions from an airbase in Thailand, where he had witnessed mongoose-cobra fights. Seeing the mongoose win again and again at the precise point at which the cobra began to rise preparing to strike, the pilot (a good Nebraskan) brought a western diamondback rattlesnake to Thailand. Because there was no snake more feared than the cobra, it was easy for him to get bets when he would pit his rattlesnake against the mongoose. And the mongoose would wait for the rattlesnake to rise up before striking. Because that was according to the rules. But the rules were foreign to the rattlesnake's nature, and the mongoose always died.

Sometimes I think of our justice system as a kind of mongoose, and I think of the chaos of legal problems as a cobra— but my cobra is a rattlesnake and my mongoose merely a beast whose duty it is to be a mongoose. I think of myself and my friends trying our best to create an approximate mongoose, knowing full well that the perfect mongoose might end up being irrelevant to the real problems we faced. I remain at a loss to define our duties, our accomplishments, and our goals in ways other than in terms of mixed and failed metaphors.

Those who would not go to Vietnam, and who have ridiculed my going, have been sanctimonious about it. And I still defend criminal cases, but each year my clients seem increasingly indignant—offended at having been caught. Those few of my friends and acquaintances who volunteered for Vietnam, hoping to do some good, are generally scorned by those who had the good sense to stay home and pile up money.

Gulliver did his best to readjust to the society he had left and adjusted so well that "I began last week to permit my wife to sit at dinner with me, at the farthest end of a long table, and to answer (but with the utmost brevity) the few questions I asked her."

But his tolerance was not without limitations: "I am not in the least provoked at the sight of a lawyer, a pick pocket, a colonel, or fool, a Lord, a gangster, a politician, a whore-master, a physician, an evidence, a suborner, an attorney, a traitor, or the like . . . but when I behold a limb of deformity and diseases both in body and mind, smitten with *pride*, it immediately breaks all the measures of my patience . . ."

Gulliver's madness and his rage were cousins to despair. Salvation lies amid the commonplace; the measured action, doing what we can.